Facts that defy belief—
yet they're all true!

Robert L. Ripley and his staff have traveled
to the farthest corners of the earth in their
continuing search for the odd and unusual, the
incredible and strange. This collection of in-
conceivable feats, wondrous sights, and apparent miracles is sure to convince you that
truth is indeed stranger than fiction.

D1287305

Ripley's Believe It or Not! titles

Ripley's Believe It or Not! 2nd Series
Ripley's Believe It or Not! 3rd Series
Ripley's Believe It or Not! 4th Series
Ripley's Believe It or Not! 5th Series
Ripley's Believe It or Not! 7th Series
Ripley's Believe It or Not! 8th Series
Ripley's Believe It or Not! 9th Series
Ripley's Believe It or Not! 10th Series
Ripley's Believe It or Not! 11th Series
Ripley's Believe It or Not! 12th Series
Ripley's Believe It or Not! 13th Series
Ripley's Believe It or Not! 14th Series
Ripley's Believe It or Not! 15th Series
Ripley's Believe It or Not! 16th Series
Ripley's Believe It or Not! 17th Series
Ripley's Believe It or Not! 18th Series
Ripley's Believe It or Not! 19th Series
Ripley's Believe It or Not! 20th Series
Ripley's Believe It or Not! 21st Series
Ripley's Believe It or Not! 22nd Series
Ripley's Believe It or Not! 23rd Series
Ripley's Believe It or Not! 24th Series
Ripley's Believe It or Not! Anniversary Edition
Ripley's Believe It or Not! Book of the Military

Published by POCKET BOOKS

Ripley's Believe It or Not!

16th Series

PUBLISHED BY POCKET BOOKS NEW YORK

RIPLEY'S BELIEVE IT OR NOT!® 16th SERIES

POCKET BOOK edition published March, 1971
5th edition........................October, 1976

This original POCKET BOOK edition is printed from brand-new
plates made from newly set, clear, easy-to-read type.
POCKET BOOK editions are published by
POCKET BOOKS,
a division of Simon & Schuster, Inc.,
A GULF+WESTERN COMPANY
630 Fifth Avenue,
New York, N.Y. 10020.
Trademarks registered in the United States
and other countries.

This is our introduction to *Ripley's Believe It Or Not! 16th Series.*

It contains a selection of all that was best in the BELIEVE IT OR NOT! newspaper feature. It also proves that we need not fear a dearth of material even on so elusive a subject as number sixteen.

On a trip to France, we were introduced to a family bearing the proud surname of Seize (sixteen). When we inquired after the origin of this family name, we were told that the original forebear was married sixteen times. Appropriately enough, their coat of arms features sixteen spinning wheels!

Among the Kasamas of Central Africa, "Sweet Sixteen" is celebrated when the celebrant is forty-four. When a child is born, it is considered to be sixty years old, the hoped-for life expectancy. Every twelve months, a year is deducted from its age. When a woman reaches the age of forty-four, she celebrates her sixteenth birthday, an important landmark in her life!

A Scottish royalist named Charles Graves had sixteen sons serving as colonels in the army of King Charles I. When this hapless monarch was executed in 1649, the sixteen Scottish colonels scattered all over Europe and engaged in the same rank in sixteen different foreign armies!

All the items in the book were researched by the undersigned, while the illustrations are the work of the distinguished BELIEVE IT OR NOT! artist Paul Frehm.

We are proud to signal the new edition sailing under the banner of number sixteen. It is a worthy successor of all that has gone before.

—Norbert Pearlroth
Research Director
BELIEVE IT OR NOT!

VILLAGES of the Jos Plateau, in Nigeria CONSIST OF ROUND HUTS LOCATED IN A CIRCLE *SO THAT THE OUTSIDE WALLS FORM A SOLID BULWARK*

HERE LIES
BENITO SANCHEZ
BUILDER OF
THIS EDIFICE
MAY GOD
FORGIVE HIM

Epitaph of the builder of the Cathedral of Ciudad Rodrigo, Spain, *WHO WAS BURIED IN THE EDIFICE IN THE 12TH CENTURY*

THE SHEPHERDS OF GULMARG in the Himalaya Mountains KEEP WARM BY WEARING BENEATH THEIR CLOTHING *A SMALL IRON STOVE*

"ABAKARU" - THE OLDEST KNOWN NAME OF A DOG WAS GIVEN TO HIS PET BY EGYPTIAN PHARAOH CHEOPS, AND THE DOG'S LIKENESS APPEARS REPEATEDLY ON THE CHEOPS PYRAMID *CONSTRUCTED MORE THAN 5,800 YEARS AGO*

THE **ÖRE** A DANISH COIN WORTH 1/8 OF A CENT, WAS NAMED AFTER THE "AUREUS" -AN ANCIENT ROMAN COIN WORTH $4.50

WOMEN of Palimbai, New Guinea, FISH BY HOLDING BETWEEN THEM A HUGE NET WHILE *PRECARIOUSLY BALANCING THEMSELVES IN THE PROWS OF 2 SMALL CANOES*

ROMANTIC YOUTHS in Arcos de La Frontera, Spain, SERENADE THEIR SWEETHEARTS THROUGH A TINY TRAPDOOR NEAR THE FLOOR OF EACH HOME - *WHICH NORMALLY SERVES AS A DOORWAY FOR THE FAMILY CAT*

THE BOWING BIRDS OF BELGIUM

FANCY SCOTTS A BREED OF BELGIAN CANARIES

ALWAYS STAND WITH THEIR HEADS BOWED DOWN ALMOST TO THEIR LEGS

THE BOSTON NATION

A NEWSPAPER PUBLISHED IN OHIO FROM 1839 TO 1841 HAD PAGES 7'6" LONG AND 5'7" WIDE - *WITH 6,000 INCHES OF READING MATTER TO A PAGE*

THE CATASTROPHE
THAT WAS A BOON
AN AVALANCHE THAT ROARED DOWN THE VALLEY OF SCHLAPPIN, IN SWITZERLAND, IN 1935, *PROVIDED RESIDENTS OF THE AREA WITH NEEDED BRIDGES OF SNOW AND EARTH ACROSS ALMOST EVERY RIVER AND BROOK*

THE POTTER WASP
TO HOLD ITS OFFSPRING *BUILDS LITTLE JUGS BY CEMENTING TOGETHER SCORES OF PEBBLES*

THE MOST GRACEFUL BRIDES IN THE WORLD
A GIRL in Vitoria, Spain, WAS NOT CONSIDERED READY FOR MARRIAGE UNTIL SHE COULD EXECUTE A WILD DANCE WITH A JUG OF WATER BALANCED ON HER HEAD *—AND NOT SPILL A SINGLE DROP!*

FISHING BOATS in Nazare, Portugal,
BECAUSE THE TOWN HAS NO HARBOR ARE HAULED ONTO SHORE WITH THEIR CATCH **BY TEAMS OF OXEN**

THE TURBANED TURK near Dambach, France NATURAL STONE FORMATION

GOVERNOR WINFIELD T. DURBIN (1847-1928) of Indiana WAS ONE OF 7 BROTHERS WHO ENLISTED IN THE UNION ARMY ON THE SAME DAY WINFIELD WAS ONLY 15 YEARS OF AGE AT THE TIME

A ROMAN WARSHIP USED IN ANCIENT TIMES TO RAM ENEMY VESSELS WAS PROPELLED BY OXEN

A MOLE, MEASURING ONLY 6 INCHES, CAN DIG A TUNNEL 100 YARDS LONG IN A SINGLE NIGHT TO PERFORM A PROPORTIONATE AMOUNT OF WORK, A MAN WOULD HAVE TO DIG A TUNNEL 50 MILES IN LENGTH

BERRIES of the Zizyphus Jujuba plant of India ARE USED TO DYE SILK IN BURMA - TO MAKE A REFRESHING SOFT DRINK IN INDIA -AND TO POISON FISH IN ETHIOPIA

LAKE ROTOMAHANA
in New Zealand
AFTER THE VOLCANIC ERUPTION
OF MOUNT TARAWERA, IN 1886,
*INCREASED TO 30 TIMES
ITS FORMER SIZE*

COLONEL SAMUEL WASHINGTON
(1734-1781)
A BROTHER
OF GEORGE
WASHINGTON
WAS
MARRIED
5
TIMES
-HAVING
BECOME
A
WIDOWER
4
TIMES

U.S. SUPREME COURT JUSTICE ROBERT GRIER
(1794-1870)
READ A CHAPTER OF THE NEW
TESTAMENT IN THE ORIGINAL GREEK
-AND TRANSLATED IT INTO ENGLISH
EVERY WEEK FOR 56 YEARS

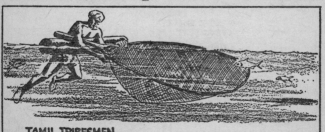

TAMIL TRIBESMEN
FISH IN THE KAVERI RIVER OF INDIA BY SPREADING A HUGE NET
WHILE FLOATING WITH THE AID OF A THICK BLOCK OF WOOD -
WHEN A FISH IS CAUGHT THEY KILL IT BY BITING OFF ITS HEAD

THE HOT HEAD

FRANÇOIS RAPHELENGE (1539-1597) PROFESSOR OF ORIENTAL LANGUAGES AT THE UNIVERSITIES OF CAMBRIDGE, ENGLAND, AND LEYDEN, HOLLAND, LECTURED WITH SUCH INTENSITY THAT DURING THE WINTER *STEAM ROSE FROM HIS HEAD*

THE STAIRWAY

BY WHICH VISITORS REACH THE 14 WATERFALLS IN AN ABYSS AT DURNAND, FRANCE, IS HALF A MILE LONG AND *IS MERELY BOLTED TO THE SHEER WALL OF THE PRECIPICE*

A COMMON TERN TAGGED IN SWEDEN ON JULY 9, 1955, WAS RECAPTURED IN FREEMANTLE, AUSTRALIA, 6 MONTHS LATER -HAVING FLOWN 13,000 MILES

THE TIGER SHARK

WHICH BEARS LIVE YOUNG MAY GIVE BIRTH TO AS MANY AS 27 INFANT SHARKS -ALL PERFECTLY FORMED AND EQUIPPED WITH TEETH

CHINCHILLAS PRODUCERS OF THE WORLD'S COSTLIEST FUR WERE EATEN BY THE CHINCHA INDIANS OF THE ANDES *IN THE BELIEF THEIR MEAT WAS A CURE-ALL FOR LUNG AILMENTS*

CLUBS WIELDED BY Bassonge tribesmen of Africa ARE CONSIDERED MOST POTENT WHEN THEY ARE CARVED IN THE LIKENESS OF A BRAVE CHIEF

FRANÇOIS-MATHIEU de BEAUCHATEAU BECAME A CELEBRATED FRENCH POET *AT THE AGE OF 8* — THEN HE VANISHED WHEN HE WAS 16 AND WAS NEVER SEEN AGAIN

A **STREET CAR** in Invercargill, New Zealand, IS PART OF THE SOUTHERNMOST TROLLEY SYSTEM IN THE WORLD AND AT ELECTION TIME DOUBLES AS A *VOTING BOOTH*

THE **PIPES** SMOKED BY BASHILANGE TRIBESMEN OF Africa ALWAYS HAVE BOWLS CARVED *TO RESEMBLE THE SMOKER*

THE **CHURCH OF SAN FRANCESCO** in Lula, Sardinia, WAS BUILT IN 1770, BY *FRANCESCO TOLU* — A BANDIT — DURING A TRIAL FOR MURDER AND ROBBERY HE HAD VOWED TO BUILD THE CHURCH IF HE WAS ACQUITTED — AND HE USED ALL HIS ILL-GOTTEN GAINS TO *CONSTRUCT THE EDIFICE*

STONE HEAD IMBEDDED IN THE WALL OF THE CHURCH OF SIMMERN IN Luxembourg ASSURED PERMANENT IMMUNITY FROM THE LAW TO ANYONE WHO TOUCHED IT

KING ERMANARICH of the Ostrogoths WHO RULED A VAST EMPIRE EXTENDING FROM THE DANUBE TO THE BALTIC COMMITTED SUICIDE IN 376 — WOUNDED BY ASSASSINS AND FACING A HUN INVASION, HE FEARED THAT HE WOULD NOT BE ABLE TO LEAD HIS TROOPS IN BATTLE AT THE AGE OF 110

THE "HEADACHE HOLE" VISITORS TO THE CHURCH OF ST. MENOUX, FRANCE, STICK THEIR HEADS IN AN APERTURE IN THE SARCOPHAGUS IN THE BELIEF IT WILL RELIEVE HEADACHES

THE SWAMP MUMMY OF WINDEBY THE BODY OF A YOUNG GIRL CONVICTED OF SORCERY AND BURIED ALIVE IN A GERMAN SWAMP WITH HER EYES BANDAGED TO PREVENT HER FROM BEWITCHING HER EXECUTIONERS WAS FOUND IN A STATE OF COMPLETE PRESERVATION — WITH EVEN THE BANDAGE INTACT — 2,000 YEARS LATER

THE **SWARKESTONE BRIDGE**
over the Trent River, England,
WAS BUILT IN 1797 BY 2 SISTERS
*WHOSE SWEETHEARTS HAD
DROWNED ATTEMPTING TO
FORD THE RIVER*

WOMEN of the
MAHRA TRIBE,
in Southern Arabia,
AS A SIGN THAT
THEY ARE MARRIED
CUT OUT A STRIP OF THEIR
SCALP ¾ OF AN INCH WIDE
FROM THEIR FOREHEAD
TO THEIR NECK

THE GREEN PLOVERS
ONE OF THE TINIEST OF BIRDS
WERE ORDERED EXTERMINATED IN 17th
CENTURY SCOTLAND BECAUSE THEIR
HABIT OF HOVERING OVER HUMANS
*BETRAYED HIDING SCOTS
TO BRITISH SOLDIERS*

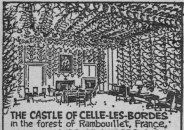

THE CASTLE OF **CELLE-LES-BORDES**
in the forest of Rambouillet, France,
HAS THOUSANDS OF ANTLERS AND
OTHER TROPHIES OF THE CHASE
*COVERING THE WALLS, CEILINGS AND
EVEN LINING THE STAIRWAYS
-OF EVERY ROOM AND HALLWAY*

THE **MUDFISH**
Protopterus annectens.
of Africa
WHEN A POND
DRIES UP
BUILDS A SHELTER
ON THE MUDDY
BOTTOM AND
*BREATHES AIR BY
USING ITS
SWIMMING BLADDER
AS A LUNG*

THE **CATHEDRAL** of **ST. ÉTIENNE** in Toulouse, France, ORIGINALLY CONSISTED OF 2 SEPARATE CHURCHES—ONE BUILT IN 1080 AND THE OTHER IN 1272 *AND NEITHER EVER COMPLETED* A WALL WAS CONSTRUCTED AROUND THEM IN 1530 TO UNITE THEM AS A SINGLE CHURCH

FEMALE TORTOISE TICKS ARE **20** TIMES AS LARGE AS THE MALE

MONTE a Tasmanian aborigine *HAD A DOUBLE SET OF TEETH* HE WOULD EXHIBIT THEM TO ANYONE WHO WOULD TOSS A COIN INTO HIS MOUTH

A **DESK** USED BY WILLIAM SHAKESPEARE AS A GRAMMAR SCHOOL STUDENT IN STRATFORD-ON-AVON

THE **OLDEST** PARISH CHURCH IN GERMANY THE CHURCH OF ST. LUCIUS in Essen-Werden HAS CONDUCTED SERVICES FOR *900 YEARS*

FARMERS of Anso, Spain, **STILL THRESH GRAIN BY MEANS OF A LARGE WOODEN SLED PULLED ACROSS THE FIELD BY A HORSE**

THE COUNT OF ARVENIE FRANKISH ARMY LEADER KILLED IN 587 WHILE ESCAPING FROM THE BURNING HOME OF THE BISHOP OF Andelot, France, WAS HIT BY SO MANY ARROWS AND LANCES THAT HE WAS *BURIED IN A VERTICAL POSITION*

A STONE CROSS in Kleinmachnow, Germany, erected in the 17th century by Georg von Hake **TO ATONE FOR THE MURDER OF A RIVAL, STILL MARKS THE SITE OF THE SLAYING** -BUT IT IS NOW PART OF THE WALL OF A STABLE

THE ALTAR of the church in the catacombs of Zaragoza, Spain, WAS ORIGINALLY AN ANCIENT COFFIN WHICH HELD *THE BODIES OF CHRISTIAN MARTYRS*

A **PREHISTORIC FOSSIL** FOUND IN SANDSTONE in Franconia, Germany, *BEARS THE SHAPE OF A HUMAN HAND*

THE REV. JOHN S. SWEENEY (1834-1908) PASTOR OF THE FIRST CHRISTIAN CHURCH OF PARIS, KY., WAS THE SON OF *A MINISTER* THE GRANDSON OF *A MINISTER* THE BROTHER OF *3 MINISTERS* AND THE FATHER OF *2 MINISTERS*

THE **TOMB** OF THE REV. STEPHEN THEODORE BADIN ON THE CAMPUS OF NOTRE DAME UNIVERSITY *IS A REPLICA OF THE LOG CABIN HE BUILT ON THE SITE 135 YEARS AGO*

A **BURNED BUS** WRECKED IN BATTLE IN WORLD WAR II STILL SERVES AS A BORDER BARRIER NEAR HELMSTEDT, GERMANY, ON A ROAD LINKING EAST AND WEST GERMANY

THE MAN WHO WAS SAVED BY A RAILROAD WRECK!

JERRY SIMPSON, WORKING ON A BRIDGE IN THE CASCADE RANGE, WASHINGTON, SAW A RUNAWAY NORTH PACIFIC ENGINE BEARING DOWN ON HIM, AND PREFERRING INSTANT DEATH TO CRIPPLING INJURY *THREW HIMSELF ACROSS ONE OF THE RAILS*

THE CAREENING ENGINE'S WHEELS ROSE FROM THE RAIL A MOMENT BEFORE HE WOULD HAVE BEEN KILLED — *AND THE ENGINE CLEARED HIS BODY AND CRASHED INTO THE GULLY BELOW* (1886)

THE **HELLBENDER**
A LARGE SALAMANDER WHICH STAYS IN THE WATER ALL ITS LIFE *HAS BOTH LUNGS AND GILLS — YET IT BREATHES ONLY THROUGH ITS SKIN*

THE **OLDEST LEGISLATOR IN HISTORY** SENATOR DAVID WARK (1804-1905) of New Brunswick, WAS STILL AN ACTIVE MEMBER OF THE SENATE IN CANADA *AT THE AGE OF 101*

THE **SNORKEL** OF THE RAT-TAILED LARVA OF THE DRONE-FLY IS **6** TIMES AS LONG AS ITS BODY

GIRLS of the Emerillon Tribe of French Guiana MUST PROVE THEY ARE READY FOR MARRIAGE BY SPENDING 5 DAYS AND NIGHTS IN A HAMMOCK WITHOUT FOOD *WHILE ENDURING THE BITES OF VICIOUS ANTS ATTRACTED TO THEM BY A TRAIL OF HONEY*

NICOLAS NOEL (1746-1832) a Frenchman WAS APPOINTED BY CONGRESS IN THE WAR OF INDEPENDENCE SURGEON GENERAL AND COMMANDER OF ALL HOSPITALS IN PHILADELPHIA, THEN RETURNED TO HIS COUNTRY AND BECAME MEDICAL INSPECTOR GENERAL OF FRANCE AND FOUNDER OF A MEDICAL COLLEGE *YET HE DID NOT RECEIVE HIS MEDICAL DEGREE UNTIL MANY YEARS LATER*

AMERICAN BANKNOTES ISSUED IN 1759 AND PRINTED BY BENJAMIN FRANKLIN *WERE BACKED BY TOBACCO INSTEAD OF GOLD*

THE **BELFRY** of the CHURCH OF ST. NICCOLÓ in Castelnuovo del Friuli, Italy, STANDS APART FROM THE EDIFICE *BECAUSE IT ORIGINALLY SERVED AS THE TOWER OF THE LOCAL CASTLE*

SETH POPE A PEDDLER OF Sandwich, Mass., WHO WAS ORDERED OUT OF TOWN BECAUSE IT WAS FEARED HE WOULD BECOME A PUBLIC CHARGE RETURNED **30** YEARS LATER *AND BOUGHT THE ENTIRE AREA*

A **GOLF BALL** DRIVEN **300** YARDS BY PRO DONALD E. DICKEN LANDED IN A KNOT-HOLE IN A TREE —COSTING HIM THE *ONE STROKE* BY WHICH HE LOST *A TOURNAMENT* Rozella Ford Golf Club Warsaw, Ind., Sept. 4, 1965

A **WOODEN NICKEL** issued in Peace River, Alberta, Canada, HONORS HENRY P. DAVIS, WHO FILED CLAIM TO *A 12-FOOT STRIP OF LAND OVERLOOKED BETWEEN 2 RICH MINES*

THE **GRAVESTONES** OF **2** SISTERS BURIED SIDE BY SIDE IN MONTMARTRE, FRANCE, — *HAVE 2 ARMS CLASPING HANDS*

THE PILE OF DIRT THAT FULFILLED A PROPHECY OF DEATH

BARCLAY, OWNER OF KILDONNAN CASTLE on the Island of Arran, Scotland, HAVING BEEN WARNED HE WOULD DIE IF HE EVER SET FOOT ON IRISH SOIL, TRIPPED ONE DAY OVER SOME CLODS OF DIRT OUTSIDE HIS CASTLE —AND UPON LEARNING THAT IT WAS BALLAST DISCARDED BY IRISH FISHERMEN *DROPPED DEAD OF FRIGHT!*

A **BUST** OF KING LOUIS IX OF France (1214-1270) in the Sainte Chapelle, Paris, HAS UNDER THE ROYAL CROWN *THE ACTUAL TOP OF THE MONARCH'S SKULL*

PAPER MONEY ISSUED IN N.Y. IN 1775 DISPLAYED ON THE BACK THE TEN COMMANDMENTS AND A NAKED SWORD, WITH THE MOTTO: *" THE LAW RULES; ARMS DEFEND"*

THE COAT OF ARMS of Lisbon, Portugal, FEATURES A SHIP AND 2 RAVENS COMMEMORATING A LEGEND THAT ST. VINCENT, PATRON SAINT OF PORTUGAL, ARRIVED IN 1137 IN A SHIP *DRAWN BY 2 RAVENS*

AN AIR TROLLEY
CARRYING WORKERS FROM SURROUNDING CLIFFS TO A DIAMOND MINE IN JOHANNESBURG, So. Africa, *RAN ON WIRE CABLES*

ELHANEN WINCHESTER BENNETT
(1823-1909) A SETTLER OF Clintonville, Wis., WAS A TRAPPER, TIMBER MERCHANT, HOTEL KEEPER, DETECTIVE, EXPLORER, SURVEYOR, DENTIST, POET, PHILANTHROPIST, VETERINARY, JUSTICE OF THE PEACE, TOWN TREASURER, ASSESSOR, SOLDIER AND INSPECTOR OF RAILROAD TRACKS AND BRIDGES

THE *ENTRANCE* TO FORT ST. CLAIR PARK, IN EATON, OHIO, IS FORMED BY 2 COLUMNS AND THE DOORWAY OF THE COMMUNITY'S OLD COURTHOUSE -ALL THE REST OF WHICH WAS DEMOLISHED YEARS AGO

EVERY CHILD
BORN ON THE ISLAND OF BALI WEARS AS A TALISMAN THROUGHOUT ITS LIFETIME *A CONTAINER IN WHICH IS PRESERVED THE INFANT'S UMBILICAL CORD*

A BRIDGE near Vandipore, Tibet, 112 FEET LONG AND ERECTED IN 1640 OF FIR BEAMS FASTENED ONLY WITH WOODEN PEGS AND NEVER PAINTED *IS STILL IN USE 3 CENTURIES LATER*

A WHITE STAG SHOT BY THE DUKE OF HESSEN in 1763 HAD A SINGLE, HUGE HORN GROWING OUT OF ONE SIDE OF ITS HEAD

HEINRICH FÜGER (1751-1818) BECAME A CELEBRATED PORTRAIT PAINTER *AT THE AGE OF 11* HE DIED AT THE AGE OF 67 AS HE APPLIED THE FINAL STROKE TO HIS LAST CANVAS *-AND FELL WITH HIS BRUSH STILL GRIPPED IN HIS FINGERS*

THE HONEY POSSUM CAN GET THE LAST BIT OF HONEY FROM A BLOSSOM *BECAUSE ITS TONGUE IS COVERED WITH BRISTLES AND ENDS IN A BRUSH OF HAIR*

THE FIRST UNDERWATER DUEL

LIEUT. WILLIAM BAILEY A DIVER IN THE BRITISH NAVY ARMED ONLY WITH A KNIFE *ENGAGED AN ITALIAN FROGMAN IN JULY, 1942,* ON THE BOTTOM OF THE STRAIT OF GIBRALTAR

HIS FOE ESCAPED WITH ONLY A RIP IN HIS RUBBER SUIT

U.S. SUPREME COURT JUSTICE **BUSHROD WASHINGTON** (1762-1829)

A NEPHEW OF GEORGE WASHINGTON, WAS BORN 30 YEARS AFTER THE BIRTH OF HIS UNCLE AND DIED 30 YEARS AFTER GEORGE WASHINGTON'S DEATH *-HAVING LIVED EXACTLY THE SAME NUMBER OF YEARS*

ENOUGH IS ENOUGH!

THE TERN FEEDS ITS YOUNG FOR AN ENTIRE YEAR AFTER THE BABIES *HAVE GROWN AS LARGE AS THEIR PARENTS*

THE OPOSSUM HAS NOT CHANGED IN 70,000,000 YEARS

THE **PEACOCK BLENNY**
(Blennius Pavo)
HAS A DOMED HEAD
THAT MAKES IT LOOK LIKE
A BALD-HEADED MAN

THE **FIRST GUIDED MISSILES**

THE **ANCIENT BRITONS**
RUBBED THE
STONES THEY
FIRED FROM THEIR
SLINGS IN THE
BRAINS OF SLAIN
ENEMIES -- IN
THE BELIEF THE
MISSILES WOULD
THUS HAVE
SUFFICIENT
BRAIN
POWER...:

...... *TO FLY
UNERRINGLY
TO THE
TARGET*

THE **ALPINE
CROWFOOT**
(Ranunculus
Alpestris)
IS THE ONLY
FLOWER
GROWING
IN THE ALPS
*AT AN ALTITUDE
OF 14,200 FEET*

THE **MALE
EMU**
ALWAYS
HATCHES
AND FEEDS
ITS YOUNG

THE **BOWLING
BALL FLUTE**
NATIVES of
Loango, Africa,
USE FLUTES
THAT ARE
*COMPLETELY
SPHERICAL*

A STREET CAR
INVENTED BY I.M.S.R. MATHEWSON
of Gilroy, Calif., in 1876
HAD ITS GASOLINE MOTOR
DISGUISED AS THE HEAD
OF A HORSE
-SO IT WOULD
NOT FRIGHTEN
REAL HORSES

THE **CHINESE HAT SNAIL**
HAS A SHELL THAT
LOOKS EXACTLY LIKE A
COOLIE'S HEADGEAR

A GIRL IN THE OVAMBO TRIBE
Africa
IS FORBIDDEN TO
PLAY WITH DOLLS
--UNTIL SHE IS
OLD ENOUGH FOR
MARRIAGE

ABORIGINE GIRLS in Australia
GATHER FRESHWATER MUSSELS *WITH THEIR TOES*-
WITHOUT TOUCHING A MUSSEL WITH THEIR HANDS. THE GIRLS SCOOP
IT UP AND DROP IT ON A BARK FLOAT

PALMER LAKE
LOCATED AT THE SUMMIT of the Continental Divide *EMPTIES BOTH NORTH AND SOUTH—* HALF OF ITS WATER FLOWS INTO THE ARKANSAS RIVER AND THE OTHER HALF INTO THE PLATTE RIVER

The **WOMAN WHO WATCHED HER OWN FUNERAL**

MARGUERITE de L'ANGLOIS, abbess of the Convent of Montmartre, in Paris, France, AWARE THAT SHE WAS DYING ON JUNE 9, 1503, ORDERED THAT HER FUNERAL BE STARTED IMMEDIATELY —*AND WAS A SPECTATOR AT THE SERVICES UNTIL HER DEATH 48 HOURS LATER*

DON LUIS ANTONIO de BORBÓN (1727-1785) BROTHER OF KING CHARLES III of Spain

BECAME A CARDINAL AT THE AGE OF 8

THE **BLACK BISKOP** a South African fish HAS A FACE THAT LOOKS LIKE THAT OF *A PUNCH-DRUNK PUG*

MONTESQUIEU
(1689-1755)

THE FRENCH PHILOSOPHER, AT HIS BAPTISM HAD AS HIS GODFATHER THE *MOST RAGGED BEGGAR HIS PARENTS COULD FIND*— THEY WANTED TO MAKE CERTAIN THAT HE WOULD ALWAYS REMEMBER THAT THE POOR WERE HIS BRETHREN

THE **24-HOUR WATCH** CARRIED BY NELLIE BLY IN 1889 *WHEN SHE MADE HER FAMED TRIP AROUND THE WORLD IN 72 DAYS*

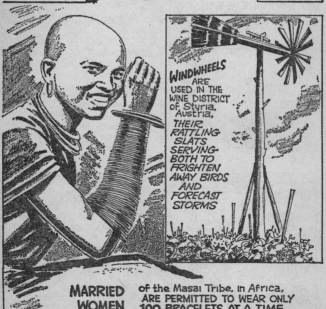

WINDWHEELS ARE USED IN THE WINE DISTRICT OF Styria, Austria, *THEIR RATTLING SLATS SERVING BOTH TO FRIGHTEN AWAY BIRDS AND FORECAST STORMS*

MARRIED WOMEN of the Masai Tribe, in Africa, ARE PERMITTED TO WEAR ONLY **100 BRACELETS AT A TIME**

MRS. BARBARA VILLONE
of Laurel, Md.,
WAS GIVEN THE SAME TELEPHONE
NUMBER~ 725-1939
AS HER DATE OF BIRTH
7/25/1939

THE **SHIELD COIN**
AN ANCIENT
CHINESE BRONZE
COIN
*COULD BE USED
ONLY FOR THE
PURCHASE OF A
WARRIOR'S SHIELD*

THE STONE MAN
AN ABORIGINE'S PROFILE
CARVED BY NATURE
the Finke Gorge, in the
MacDonnell Mountain Range,
Central Australia

**CRUDE
MEMORIALS**
erected in
neighboring
communities
in Poland
ONE HONORING
A MONK KILLED
BY A WOLF IN
FLORIANSDORF
AND THE OTHER
MARKING THE
SPOT IN MARKSDORF
*WHERE THE ANIMAL
WAS KILLED*

THE **TEETOTALER** WHO DIED OF "ALCOHOLISM"
DUKE ANTONIO FERDINANDO
ruler of Guastalla, Italy, from 1714 to 1729,
NEVER TOOK A DRINK BECAUSE A SOOTHSAYER
WARNED THAT ALCOHOL WOULD KILL HIM
ON APRIL 19, 1729, THE DUKE RUBBED HIS
ACHING MUSCLES WITH ALCOHOL AFTER
A HUNTING TRIP, CAUGHT FIRE
– AND BURNED TO DEATH!

**THE INK
MUSHROOM**
(Coprinus)
DISINTEGRATES
INTO A DARK
LIQUID THAT
*LOOKS JUST
LIKE INK*

THE **CASTLE THAT WAS WORTH A KINGDOM**
QUEEN CATHERINE of Cyprus TRADED
HER ENTIRE KINGDOM TO VENICE FOR
THE CHATEAU OF OSOLO, ITALY – 1498

THIS HUSBAND IS A REAL BIRD
THE MALE VERDIN SPENDS EACH DAY IN HIS WIFE'S NEST BUT *SLEEPS EVERY NIGHT IN HIS OWN NEST*

THE MOST COURAGEOUS MOTHER IN HISTORY
SOPHIA ZINKNAGEL, WIFE OF A SERGEANT IN NAPOLEON'S ARMY, GAVE BIRTH TO A BABY WHILE ACCOMPANYING HER HUSBAND ON THE ILL-FATED INVASION OF RUSSIA IN 1812, AND DURING THE FRENCH RETREAT, IN TEMPERATURES AS LOW AS 30° BELOW ZERO, *SHE WALKED 1200 MILES FROM MOSCOW TO HER NATIVE HALLE, GERMANY, WITH THE INFANT IN HER ARMS*

HER HUSBAND DIED ON THE JOURNEY AND SHE HAD NO WARM CLOTHING FOR THE BABY — YET *SHE BROUGHT THE CHILD HOME SAFELY*

KITTEN
BORN WITH ONLY 3 LEGS

Berries of the Dwarf Mistletoe *TAKE ROOT ONLY BY BEING EXPLODED INTO THE LIMB OF ANOTHER TREE* THEY ARE CATAPULTED WITH SUCH FORCE THAT THE BERRIES OFTEN LAND ON A TREE 60 FEET AWAY

A TABLE KNIFE
DESIGNED IN THE 16th century *TO TEACH THE USER TO HOLD IT TIGHTLY WHILE CARVING*
IF HIS GRIP SLACKENED, A DOOR OPENED IN THE HANDLE AND A TINY FIGURE EMERGED

3 BOMBS THROWN AT THE CARRIAGE OF *EMPEROR NAPOLEON III* of France *KILLED OR WOUNDED EVERY ONE OF THE 156 MEN IN HIS HONOR GUARD—YET THE EMPEROR AND HIS EMPRESS ESCAPED HARM* (Jan. 14, 1858)

THE **CRANE FLY** IS AIDED IN GLIDING THROUGH THE AIR BY THE FACT THAT ITS LEGS ARE HOLLOW AND CONTAIN SACS AND TUBES *FILLED WITH AIR*

THE **OFFICIAL EXECUTIONER** of Lyon, France, from 1760 to 1770 AN EXPERT AT HANGINGS, BEHEADINGS, BONE BREAKING AND FLOGGING WAS CAMILLE RACCOURSE —*A WOMAN MASQUERADING AS A MAN !*

THE CURTAIN TREE
near Yungaburra, Australia,
A FIG TREE COVERED FROM
CROWN TO ROOTS BY A
DENSE CURTAIN OF BRANCHES

MADRENA
A FAMED
VENETIAN COURTESAN
of the 16th century
MEMORIZED ALL THE
WRITINGS OF BOTH
*PETRARCH AND
BOCCACCIO*

THE **BATTLE
FORMATION**
OF THE ZULUS,
of Africa
BECAUSE THEY
RESPECTED THE
FIGHTING PROWESS
OF THEIR CATTLE
*WAS ALWAYS IN THE
SHAPE OF A COW'S HORNS*

THE **TOMBSTONE**
in the Church of St. Martin,
in Eisenstadt, Austria,
OVER THE GRAVE OF A TIN
MAGNATE NAMED FURST
IS MADE ENTIRELY OF TIN

THE **NEST**
OF THE
HAMMER-
HEAD BIRD
IS BUILT
IN 3 TIERS
*AND IS
STRONG-
ENOUGH TO
SUPPORT
THE WEIGHT
OF A MAN*

THE KEYHOLE HOUSE

A HOME near Lenoir, N.C.,
BUILT IN 1818 BY GEORGE POWELL
WHO WAS SO SUPERSTITIOUS HE
CONSTRUCTED A KEYHOLE OPENING
NEAR THE TOP OF THE CHIMNEY
AS AN EXIT FOR WITCHES

SIR JOHN ROYDS
(1752-1817)
JUSTICE OF THE SUPREME
COURT OF BENGAL, INDIA,
DYING IN 1810 OF A DISEASE
THAT COULD NOT BE DIAGNOSED,
WAS PRESCRIBED BY HIS DOCTOR,
AS A LAST-RESORT MEDICATION,
*4 BOTTLES OF CLARET
EVERY 24 HOURS*
SIR JOHN WAS GIVEN
28 BOTTLES OF CLARET
*-AND SURVIVED
ANOTHER 7 YEARS*

The COUNTESS de GENLIS
1746-1830
French author of 149 books
CONSIDERED IT IMMORAL FOR A
LIBRARY TO DISPLAY BOOKS
BY MEN AND WOMEN WRITERS
ON THE SAME SHELVES

A **MASK**
IS ALWAYS
WORN BY
DANCERS OF
the Ogowe
Tribe of Africa
*TO PREVENT
ANYONE FROM
"STEALING"
THEIR FACE
WHILE THEY
GYRATE IN
A TRANCE*

THE **HOUSE** OF THE FAUN
IN BURIED POMPEII,
THE MOST ARISTOCRATIC
DWELLING IN THAT CITY, HAD
4 DINING ROOMS - *ONE FOR EACH SEASON OF THE YEAR*

ADOLPHUS KOEPPEN
(1804 - 1873)
A PROFESSOR AT FRANKLIN AND
MARSHALL COLLEGE, IN LANCASTER, PA.,
*DONNED EVENING CLOTHES TWICE A
DAY - FOR LUNCH AND DINNER -
THROUGHOUT HIS ADULT LIFE*

THE PENITENTS
the Andes Mountains, in Chile,
A MYSTERIOUS FORMATION
OF ICE AND SNOW

THE **CHAPEL OF SANT BENET**
IS THE ONLY TRACE REMAINING OF THE VILLAGE OF VILA de MONT,
SPAIN - *ALL THE REST OF WHICH WAS DESTROYED 400 YEARS AGO*

THE **CHURCH** OF OUR LADY OF PEACE
in Treignac, France,
THE ONLY FRENCH CHURCH
TO BEAR THAT NAME
WAS CONVERTED INTO A TOWN
HALL AND A COURTHOUSE DURING
THE FRENCH REVOLUTION AND
STILL SERVES THE COMMUNITY
175 YEARS LATER

THE **MAN WHO LEFT A DAILY**
TRAIL OF GOOD DEEDS
Chelebi Arditi
a banker of Ismir, Turkey,
PLACED 50 PIASTERS IN
SMALL CHANGE IN HIS
POCKET EACH MORNING
AND ALLOWED THE COINS
TO TRICKLE OUT OF A
HOLE AS HE WALKED

GASTON
DOUMERGUE
(1863-1937)
AMASSED
NO WEALTH
WHILE
SERVING AS
PRESIDENT
OF FRANCE
FROM 1924
TO 1931

—BUT A
LOTTERY
TICKET HE
PURCHASED
UPON
RETURNING
TO PRIVATE
LIFE
WON HIM
$100,000

THE **FLEA CRAB** (*Niphargus aquilex*) FOUND IN DEEP WELLS IN WHICH THERE IS NO LIGHT HAS *NEITHER PIGMENT NOR EYES*

A **WOMAN** OF THE Kunama Tribe of Eritrea WEARS HER WEDDING RING *IN HER NOSE*

THE FIRST JET-POWERED VEHICLE

THE **EOLIPILE**, A VEHICLE THAT RAN ON 3 WHEELS, WAS DRIVEN FORWARD BY THE BACKPRESSURE OF STEAM ESCAPING FROM A WATER-FILLED METAL BALL HEATED BY AN ALCOHOL LAMP **99 YEARS AGO**

THE **ASPARAGUS BEETLE** HAS ON ITS WINGS *A DOUBLE CROSS*

PHILORTH

A RAILROAD STATION IN SCOTLAND WAS MAINTAINED BY THE GREAT NORTH OF SCOTLAND RAILWAY EXCLUSIVELY *FOR THE USE OF LORD SALTOUN FOR 58 YEARS*

JEAN RESTOU (1663-1702) famed French painter
WAS THE SON OF A PAINTER
GRANDSON OF A PAINTER
HUSBAND OF A PAINTER
FATHER OF A PAINTER
BROTHER OF 9 PAINTERS
AND GRANDFATHER
OF 2 PAINTERS

THE AFRICAN PIG FROG
WHEN FRIGHTENED
CAN BLOW
ITSELF UP TO
LOOK LIKE
A SMALL PIG

ANTOINE RENOU (1731-1806)
FAMED AS A FRENCH POET, PAINTER AND PLAYWRIGHT
*FOR 40 YEARS DIVIDED HIS WORKING DAY INTO 3 SHIFTS
AND DEVOTED 3 HOURS TO EACH OF HIS ARTISTIC LABORS*
HE SAID THAT PAINTING WAS THE MOST DEMANDING EFFORT

THE **CORPSES** of Tasmanian aborigines WERE PLACED IN FRAGILE TENTS OF BARK -SO THEY WOULD EVENTUALLY BE LOST TO THE ELEMENTS

JOHN HENLEY
(1692-1756) a London preacher
WROTE A GRAMMAR
IN 10 LANGUAGES

- SPANISH, FRENCH, GREEK, ITALIAN, LATIN, CHALDEAN, HEBREW, ARAMAIC, GERMAN AND PORTUGUESE

CHILDREN of the Anyuau Tribe of Ethiopia, WHEN SWIMMING IN THE BARO RIVER, ALWAYS JOIN HANDS TO FORM A "V," SPLASH AND SHOUT -IN THE BELIEF THAT BY IMPERSONATING A SEA MONSTER THEY WILL FRIGHTEN AWAY CROCODILES

MARIN-NOEL des VERGERS
(1759-1836) a Justice of the Commercial Court of Paris, France, WAS PROMOTED TO THE PRESIDENCY OF THE COURT 20 TIMES —AND 20 TIMES *REFUSED THE HONOR*

BIRTHDAY COINS
EXCHANGED BY THE ANCIENT CHINESE AS GIFTS TO MARK THEIR EMPEROR'S BIRTHDAY BORE THE INSCRIPTION: *"10,000 YEARS OF LONG LIFE.."*

AN ENGRAVED BRONZE BUCKET
USED BY ANCIENT MAN IN 700 B.C. AS A HOUSEHOLD UTENSIL *WAS USED ALSO AS THE FUNERAL URN TO HOLD HIS ASHES*

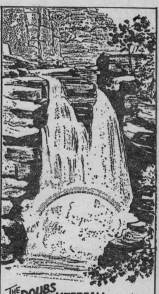

THE DOUBS WATERFALL on the border of France and Switzerland
164 FEET HIGH HAS A PERMANENT RAINBOW *THAT IS VISIBLE WHENEVER THE SUN SHINES* BUT IT CAN BE SEEN IN THE VAPOR AROUND THE WATERFALL *ONLY WHEN THE VIEWER STANDS WITH HIS BACK TO THE SUN*

THE CITY OF THE BIRDS

KIANG HSEN
an ancient city in Burma
HAS VANISHED EXCEPT FOR THE
RUINS OF ITS 53 TEMPLES
-WHICH HAVE BEEN PREVENTED
FROM DISINTEGRATING BY BIRDS-
THE BIRDS DROPPED THE SEEDS
OF PEEPAL TREES AND A TREE
GROWS ATOP THE RUIN OF
EACH TEMPLE -WHICH IS HELD
TOGETHER BY THE ROOTS OF ITS TREE

GIRLS of Bali

UNTIL THEY REACH THE AGE OF 7
MUST HAVE SHAVEN HEADS
THEY WEAR WIGS MADE
OF PALM FIBERS

NOON

SUNRISE

A SHADOW CLOCK

CONSISTING OF A
SHORT PIECE OF WOOD
POINTING EASTWARD, WHICH
CAST ITS SHADOW ON A
LONGER BOARD ON WHICH
WERE MARKED OFF THE HOURS
FROM SUNRISE TO NOON -USED
IN EGYPT 3,400 YEARS AGO

THE ENTIRE DOORWAY

OF THE TEMPLE OF
MACHENDRANATH, NEPAL,
IS BUILT OF
SOLID SILVER

THE OLD VINCENNES UNIVERSITY in Vincennes, Ind., IN THE YEARS BETWEEN 1839 AND 1884 SERVED SUCCESSIVELY AS A COLLEGE A BOYS' SCHOOL A GIRLS' SCHOOL AN ORPHANAGE A HOSPITAL A POORHOUSE A SEMINARY AND A GIRLS' HIGH SCHOOL

THE "REALISTIC EYES" ON THE WINGS OF THE PEACOCK BUTTERFLY FRIGHTEN OFF PREDATORS AND ALSO INCREASE FLIGHT EFFICIENCY BY INCREASING THE ABSORPTION OF HEAT AND IMPROVING THE CIRCULATION OF BLOOD AND AIR

NUBIAN TROOPS in the ancient Egyptian army AS THEIR REGIMENTAL INSIGNIA WORE THE TAILS OF 2 CATS -ONE TIED TO THE WAIST AND THE OTHER HANGING FROM ONE KNEE

THE WOLF FISH of Iceland WHICH ATTAINS A LENGTH OF 6 FEET HAS TEETH SO STRONG THAT IT CAN CRUSH A FULLY GROWN LOBSTER OR CRAB AND THE LARGEST OF WHELK SHELLS

YOUNG BOYS

of the Aranda Tribe of Central Australia ARE RECOGNIZED AS MEN ONLY AFTER THEY HAVE *LAIN FOR SEVERAL MINUTES ON BRANCHES SPREAD OVER A BLAZING FIRE*

SIR JAMES MELVILLE

TO NOTIFY QUEEN ELIZABETH I OF THE BIRTH OF A SON TO MARY STUART RODE FROM EDINBURGH TO LONDON *TRAVELING 400 MILES IN 3 DAYS —ALL ON THE SAME HORSE* THE BABY BECAME KING JAMES I OF ENGLAND (1566)

THE MARKET CHURCH

of Essen, Germany, DESTROYED BY ALLIED BOMBS IN WORLD WAR II, WAS FOUND TO HAVE BEEN STANDING ON GROUND SO WEAKENED BY 3 COAL MINES DUG BENEATH IT THAT *IT WOULD HAVE COLLAPSED*

THE BALANCING BOULDER of BRANDIS near Castellane, France, AN OBELISK-80 FEET HIGH-TOPPED BY A BOULDER SO LOOSELY BALANCED *THAT IT SWAYS IN THE WIND-* YET IT HAS ENDURED FOR CENTURIES

PRINCESS de LAMBALLE
(1749-1792)
CLOSEST FRIEND AND CELLMATE OF MARIE ANTOINETTE, WAS GUILLOTINED BEFORE THE QUEEN, HER HEAD WAS CARRIED BY THE MOB TO A BEAUTY PARLOR, AND THE HAIR COIFFURED AS SHE ALWAYS WORE IT—
THEN THE HEAD WAS LIFTED TO MARIE ANTOINETTE'S WINDOW TO FURTHER TERRIFY HER

ARABI CAVE in Yecla, Spain, HAS IN ITS ENTRANCEWAY THE PERFECT PROFILE OF A MAN -*CARVED BY NATURE*

QUAKING GRASS IS KNOWN BY 69 NAMES IN ENGLISH -AND 150 DIFFERENT NAMES IN GERMAN

A **TALL TREE** HAS BEEN GROWING NEAR ULIVETO, Italy, INSIDE A LARGE CAVERN *FOR 100 YEARS*

A **GIRL** in Montehermoso, Spain, REVEALS THAT SHE IS STILL SINGLE *BY WEARING A MIRROR IN HER HAT*— WIDOWS REPLACE THE MIRROR REMOVED WHEN THEY MARRIED *—BUT SHATTER ITS REFLECTING SURFACE*

A SPANISH MACKEREL HOOKED IN THE GULF OF MEXICO BY PAUL STEVEN OF BATON ROUGE, LA., *WAS WEARING A PLASTIC RING*

WEDDED TREES

THE WEDDED TREES YELLOWSTONE NATIONAL PARK

A **HUGE TOTEM POLE** on Treasure Island, San Francisco, Calif., WAS CARVED BY DUDLEY C. CARTER *FROM A SINGLE GIANT TREE*

WILLIAM MONTGOMERY (1869-1955) WAS SECRETARY OF A LIFE INSURANCE COMPANY, in Washington, D.C. *FOR 62 YEARS*

THE **ROMAN LEAP YEAR** HAD ONE DAY—FEB. 23— *WHICH LASTED 48 HOURS*

BEACON HILL in Worcestershire, England, ONLY 1,395 FEET HIGH *OVERLOOKS 15 COUNTIES*

THE **LACE WING**, AN INSECT, LAYS ONE BATCH OF EGGS ON A LEAF AND THEN BALANCES ITS NEXT EGGS ON THIN FILAMENTS ABOVE THEM *SO THE OFFSPRING HATCHED FIRST WILL NOT BE ABLE TO DEVOUR THE NEW EGGS*

The BAOBAB

A TREE WITH A TRUNK 30 FEET IN DIAMETER *GROWS HORIZONTALLY ONLY ON THE PENINSULA OF CAP-VERT, AFRICA* UNUSUAL CHEMICALS IN THE SOIL AT CAP-VERT ARE BELIEVED RESPONSIBLE

A SINGLE CITIZEN

of Oggersheim, Germany, REMAINED BEHIND WHEN ALL OTHER INHABITANTS FLED AT THE APPROACH OF A SPANISH ARMY IN 1630 AND, PRETENDING HE WAS NEGOTIATING FOR AN ENTIRE GARRISON, SURRENDERED ONLY AFTER EXACTING A PROMISE *TO SPARE ALL LIFE AND PROPERTY*

CALANDRELLA RAZAE

a small lark BREEDS ONLY WITHIN AN AREA OF 3 SQUARE MILES *ON THE ISLAND OF RAZO, IN THE CAPE VERDE ISLANDS*

The CHURCH of ST. PAUL

in Karuizawa, Japan, WAS BUILT ENTIRELY FROM *MATERIAL FOUND ON ITS SITE* CEDAR GROWING ON THE SPOT PROVIDED THE WOOD AND THE CONCRETE WAS MADE FROM LAVA DUG FROM THE GROUND

@UEEN SIGRID STORRADE of Denmark ORDERED KING HAROLD GRAENSKA OF NORWAY SLAIN - *BECAUSE HE HAD THE TEMERITY TO PROPOSE MARRIAGE*

A PAIR OF IRON BELLS JOINED BY A HANDLE OF PALM STEMS IS USED BY THE BWAKA TRIBE OF AFRICA AS *CURRENCY IN THE PURCHASE OF A WIFE*

THE **SECRETIVE WOMEN** OF **SANA'A** Yemen

WOMEN IN SANA'A *WEAR 3 VEILS UNDER THEIR HOODS*

The APUIZEIRO TREE IN THE CEMETERY OF Candelaria, Brazil, SERVES AS A TOMBSTONE OVER THE GRAVE OF A MAN WHOSE NAME WAS APUIZEIRO

The WHIRLING WINDMILL of ZAUCHWITZ In Germany TURNS WITH THE WIND SO THAT ITS VANES ALWAYS FACE IN THE RIGHT DIRECTION

A BULLFIGHT IS STAGED ANNUALLY In Garrovillas, Spain, IN THE PLAZA IN THE HEART OF THE CITY—BUT A TENT-LIKE STRUCTURE IS ERECTED AS A PLACE OF REFUGE FOR THE TOREROS

from an old print

BATTLESHIPS
CONSTRUCTED IN THE 14th CENTURY
WHEN FIREARMS HAD NOT YET
BEEN PROVED EFFECTIVE
COMPRISED 2 VESSELS JOINED
BY A SUPERSTRUCTURE
-ONE MANNED BY MARINES WITH
GUNS AND THE OTHER BY ARCHERS

YAMANA TRIBESMEN
of the Cape Horn Archipelago
AS A SIGN OF MOURNING
*SCRATCH THEIR FACES
WITH THEIR FINGERNAILS-*
THEY TEAR THE SKIN IN
DIFFERENT DESIGNS TO
REVEAL WHETHER THE DEATH
WAS OF NATURAL CAUSES,
VIOLENCE OR ACCIDENT

A BROKEN SKI
FOUND IN A SWAMP
in southern Norway
*WAS CONSTRUCTED
2,500 YEARS AGO*

SERAFINO GONZAGA
WAS A MEMBER OF THE RULING
FAMILY OF MANTUA, ITALY,
YET WHEN HE WAS CONVICTED OF
WRITING A LIBELOUS STATEMENT IN 1517
HE WAS PUNISHED BY HAVING THE
4 FINGERS WITH WHICH HE PENNED
THE LIBEL **CHOPPED OFF!**

A **CHINESE COIN** CAST 1,800 YEARS AGO WAS SHAPED LIKE A MAGIC MIRROR IN THE BELIEF IT WOULD ASSURE *LUCKY INVESTMENTS*

NANTHA AN OLD WOMAN OF Lhasa, Tibet, *CLAIMED TO BE 150 YEARS OF AGE*

BEAVER ROCK NATURAL STONE FORMATION Lake LeBarge, Yukon Territory

THE **WATER BOATMAN** DEPOSITS ITS EGGS *ON THE SHELL OF A CRAYFISH* THE GILLS OF THE CRAYFISH AERATE THE EGGS

CARP and **PARROT FISH** *CHEW THEIR FOOD* THEY HAVE TEETH IN THEIR THROAT

THE **MONDEGO** RIVER IS THE ONLY ONE IN PORTUGAL THAT *HAS ITS SOURCE IN PORTUGAL* ALL THE OTHER PORTUGUESE RIVERS ORIGINATE IN SPAIN

THE SATIN BOWER BIRD of Australia PAINTS THE INSIDE OF ITS NEST WITH CHARCOAL

MOUNTAIN CLIMBERS

MUST CLAMBER UP THE STEEP CLIFFS OVERHANGING THE ALPINE HIGHWAY, IN BAVARIA, EACH SPRING *TO DISLODGE ROCKS LOOSENED BY THE THAW*

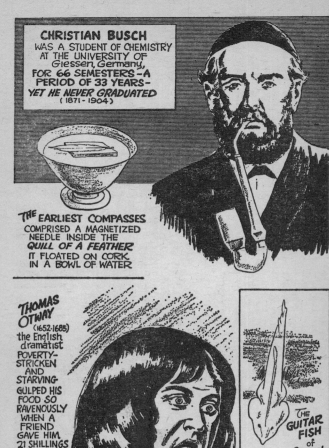

CHRISTIAN BUSCH
WAS A STUDENT OF CHEMISTRY
AT THE UNIVERSITY OF
Giessen, Germany,
FOR 66 SEMESTERS —A
PERIOD OF 33 YEARS—
YET HE NEVER GRADUATED
(1871 - 1904)

THE EARLIEST COMPASSES
COMPRISED A MAGNETIZED
NEEDLE INSIDE THE
QUILL OF A FEATHER
IT FLOATED ON CORK
IN A BOWL OF WATER

THOMAS OTWAY
(1652-1685)
the English
dramatist
POVERTY-
STRICKEN
AND
STARVING
GULPED HIS
FOOD SO
RAVENOUSLY
WHEN A
FRIEND
GAVE HIM
21 SHILLINGS
*THAT HE
CHOKED
TO DEATH
ON THE
FIRST
BITE*

THE
*GUITAR
FISH*
of
Senegal,
Africa,

ACTUALLY
IS SHAPED
LIKE THE
MUSICAL
INSTRUMENT

A
TOTEM POLE
100 FEET HIGH
ERECTED IN WINDSOR GREAT PARK England
TO CELEBRATE THE CENTENARY OF BRITISH COLUMBIA
WEIGHS 13½ TONS AND WAS CARVED FROM A *SINGLE TREE 600 YEARS OLD*

PASTOR HERMAN AUGUSTUS WINTER
A FOUNDER OF LAKELAND COLLEGE, IN SHEBOYGAN, WIS., *ALSO FOUNDED 22 CONGREGATIONS OF THE GERMAN REFORMED CHURCH*

A **DUCK** THAT WILL LAY EGGS ONLY *IN A PAN OF WATER*

THE *STONE CAMEL* CARVED BY NATURE
Woodward Cave, Woodward, Pa.

MEMORIAL TO A BANDIT

THE LIKENESS OF BLACK JACK KETCHUM, RAILROAD BANDIT AND MURDERER, CHISELED BY AN UNKNOWN SCULPTOR IN A HUGE BOULDER NEAR CIMARRON, N.M. KETCHUM WAS HANGED IN CLAYTON, N.M., IN 1901

THE STRANGEST FISHING NETS IN THE WORLD

NETS used by New Guinea fishermen *ACTUALLY ARE SPIDER WEBS* THE WEBS, WOVEN BY SPIDERS ON BAMBOO FRAMES LEFT IN THE JUNGLE, SHED WATER AND CAN BE USED FOR YEARS

AMBER HALL

IN THE IMPERIAL PALACE IN LENINGRAD, RUSSIA, HAD ITS CEILINGS AND WALLS COVERED WITH AMBER –A GIFT TO CZAR PETER THE GREAT FROM KING FREDERICK WILLIAM OF PRUSSIA –*IN RETURN FOR 55 VERY TALL RUSSIANS FOR THE PRUSSIAN RULER'S ELITE GUARD REGIMENT*

THE **MILL** of West Ashling, England, CAN BE OPERATED BY *WATER, WIND OR STEAM*

MEN of the Akha Tribe of Northern Thailand WEAR A SHORT QUEUE *IN THE BELIEF IT KEEPS THEIR SANITY FROM LEAKING AWAY*

THE STRANGEST TIDE IN THE WORLD AN UNDERGROUND LAKE IN THE SANDSTONE CAVES OF VALKENBURG, HOLLAND, *RISES AND FALLS EVERY 7 YEARS*

THE **MOST PRIZED SOUVENIR** SOUGHT BY VISITORS TO Cremona, Italy, HOMETOWN OF THE FAMED VIOLINMAKER, *IS A MINIATURE COPY OF A STRADIVARIUS*

ÉTIENNE CROPT
(1798-1896)

PROFESSOR OF LAW AT THE SCHOOL OF SION, Switzerland, *WAS THE SCHOOL'S ENTIRE FACULTY FOR 71 YEARS*

HE LECTURED FOR 4 HOURS DAILY 9 MONTHS OF EACH YEAR – AND ALSO SERVED AS PRESIDENT OF THE LOCAL COURT FOR 50 YEARS

A *SPECIAL* DELIVERY STAMP ISSUED IN CHINA IN 1905 *MEASURED 8¼ BY 2½ INCHES*

IT CONSISTED OF 4 DETACHABLE PARTS, ONE KEPT BY THE SENDER AS A RECEIPT, ONE HELD IN THE ISSUING POST OFFICE, ONE USED AS THE ACTUAL STAMP, AND THE FINAL PART RETAINED IN THE POST OFFICE TO WHICH IT WAS SENT

LANDRU
THE FRENCH MASS MURDERER WHO WAS CONVICTED OF SLAYING 11 WOMEN BECAME SO POPULAR DURING HIS TRIAL THAT IN THE FRENCH GENERAL ELECTION OF NOV. 16, 1919 *4000 VOTES WERE CAST FOR HIM FOR VARIOUS OFFICES*

A **DECOY DUCK** found in the Love Lock Caves, Nevada, HAD BEEN MADE OF RUSHES BY INDIANS SEVERAL CENTURIES AGO

A **LOCOMOTIVE** FOUND ON AN ABANDONED TRACK IN BRAZIL IN 1907 WAS RESTORED TO SERVICE ALTHOUGH IT HAD STOOD IN THE JUNGLE FOR 30 YEARS AND A TREE WAS GROWING OUT OF ITS SMOKESTACK

WARRIORS of Mindimbit, New Guinea, ALWAYS CARRY A STICK FROM WHICH IS SUSPENDED A PENDANT FOR EACH ENEMY SLAIN IN BATTLE

THE **MOSQUITO FERN** (*Azolla caroliniana*) ALWAYS SHELTERS ANOTHER PLANT —BLUE GREEN ALGA— YET IT GETS NO APPARENT BENEFIT FROM ITS TENANT

A **SUNDIAL** in Basel, Switzerland, MEASURES 33 FEET IN DIAMETER AND *USES A LIVE MAN AS ITS POINTER* HE STEPS ON THE APPROPRIATE MONTH ON A CALENDAR BOARD AND HIS SHADOW INDICATES THE TIME

JAMES B. WILLIAMS of Dover, Del., WAS A LEAP-YEAR BABY —BORN ON FEB. 29, 1944— AND BECAME THE FATHER OF A LEAP-YEAR BABY ON FEB. 29, 1968

EDWIN M. STANTON (1814-1869) WAS COMMISSIONED A U.S. SUPREME COURT JUSTICE 5 WEEKS AFTER HIS DEATH

STANTON DIED 4 DAYS AFTER THE U.S. SENATE APPROVED HIS NOMINATION, BUT PRESIDENT GRANT SENT STANTON'S COMMISSION TO HIS WIDOW ON FEB. 1, 1870 —ON THE DAY HIS APPOINTMENT WAS TO HAVE TAKEN EFFECT

THE STONE GATE ON THE ROAD BETWEEN WEGGIS AND KALTBAD SWITZERLAND, WAS FORMED BY 4 HUGE ROCKS THAT ROLLED DOWN THE MOUNTAIN —AND FORMED A PERFECT GATEWAY

THE **OPOSSUM SHRIMP**
HAS ITS EARS IN ITS TAIL

GENERAL **DELAUNAY** (1738-1825)
ENLISTED IN THE FRENCH
ARMY AT 16 AND SERVED
IT FOR A PERIOD OF
61 YEARS

PUEBLO VIEJO
a town in Venezuela,
IS BUILT ENTIRELY ON
STILTS OVER THE WATERS
OF LAKE MARACAIBO

CAPTAIN HERMAN LEMAIRE

AFTER LOSING A LEG IN THE
NAPOLEONIC RETREAT FROM MOSCOW,
DELIVERED SECRET DISPATCHES TO
NAPOLEON BY DRESSING HIMSELF
IN BEGGAR'S CLOTHING AND, ON
A HASTILY FITTED WOODEN LEG,
WALKING FROM HAMBURG,
GERMANY, TO PARIS, FRANCE, A
DISTANCE OF 600 MILES (1812)

THE **POTTO**
a lemuroid of Western Africa,
CLOWNS BY STICKING OUT ITS
TONGUE, *AND EVEN WINKS*

A **WARRIOR'S GRAVE**
in Satami, Assam,
HAS SUSPENDED OVER IT
BASKET-WEAVE GLOBES AND
POTS - *ONE FOR EACH
ENEMY HE HAS SLAIN*

**ABSENT-MINDED
PROFESSOR**
PROF. OTTO GRADENWITZ
(1860-1935)
WHO TAUGHT ROMAN
AND CIVIL LAW AT
THE UNIVERSITY OF
Heidelberg, Germany,
FOUND IT SO DIFFICULT TO
REMEMBER APPOINTMENTS
*THAT HE ALWAYS MAILED
HIMSELF A POSTCARD
LISTING HIS SCHEDULE
FOR THE FOLLOWING DAY*

**STONE
HEAD**
CARVED BY NATURE
Serra da Estrela,
Portugal

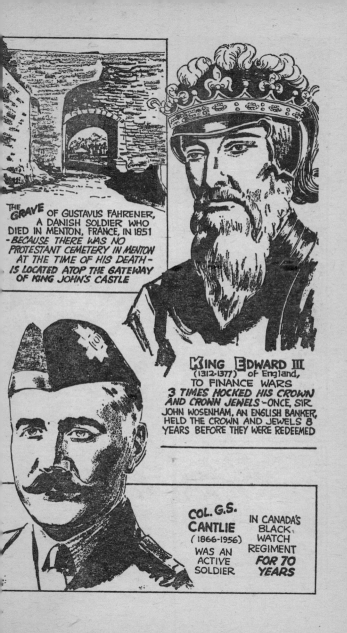

THE *GRAVE* OF GUSTAVUS FAHRENER, A DANISH SOLDIER WHO DIED IN MENTON, FRANCE, IN 1851 -*BECAUSE THERE WAS NO PROTESTANT CEMETERY IN MENTON AT THE TIME OF HIS DEATH*- IS LOCATED ATOP THE GATEWAY OF *KING JOHN'S CASTLE*

KING EDWARD III
(1312-1377) of England,
TO FINANCE WARS
3 TIMES HOCKED HIS CROWN AND CROWN JEWELS -ONCE, SIR JOHN WOSENHAM, AN ENGLISH BANKER, HELD THE CROWN AND JEWELS 8 YEARS BEFORE THEY WERE REDEEMED

COL. G.S. CANTLIE (1866-1956) WAS AN ACTIVE SOLDIER IN CANADA'S BLACK WATCH REGIMENT *FOR 70 YEARS*

AN **ANCIENT GATE** 600 YEARS OLD
IS PRESERVED INSIDE THE CHURCH
of St. Paul, in Dax, France,
AS A MEMORIAL TO THE
ORIGINAL CHURCH WHICH WAS
DEMOLISHED 300 YEARS AGO

MINIATURE CHAPELS
SHELTERING TINY HOUSEHOLD
GODS WERE PLACED IN THE
HOMES OF THE WEALTHY
IN ANCIENT ROME—
*WHEN THE OWNER DIED THE CHAPEL
WAS BURIED WITH HIM*

THE **SWORD-BILL
HUMMINGBIRD**
HAS A BILL
*LONGER
THAN ITS
BODY*

THE **NECKLACED
LAUGHING THRUSH**
of India
DISPLAYS ON ITS BREAST
WHAT APPEARS TO BE
*A NECKLACE OF
BLACK PEARLS*

GIACOMO MEYERBEER
(1791-1864)
THE FAMOUS COMPOSER OF
GRAND OPERAS SUMMERED
FOR 33 YEARS AT SPA, BELGIUM,
AND EACH DAY WENT DONKEY
RIDING—SEATED SIDEWAYS
IN A WICKER BASKET

THE STONE BAROMETER
MOUNT PILATUS (Switzerland)
6,996 FEET HIGH
HAS A CLOUD ABOVE ITS
PEAK WHEN FAIR WEATHER
IMPENDS, BUT WHEN LONG
CLOUD STRIPS ARE SEEN
ALONGSIDE ITS SLOPES
*THE NATIVES ALWAYS
PREPARE FOR A STORM*

SEBASTIAN **CROLL**
Governor of Fort Orange - now Albany, N.Y. -
INTRODUCED TO THE NEW WORLD
THE CRULLER
-WHICH WAS NAMED IN HIS HONOR

THE
LEAF-
FISH
FLOATS ON THE SURFACE OF
THE WATER AND RESEMBLES
A BOBBING LEAF

AN IRON HORSESHOE
8 FEET HIGH,
WAS ERECTED AS THE GATE
TO THE BRIDLE PATH AT
St. Leonhard im Buchet, Bavaria,
*BY A HORSEBACK RIDER
GRATEFUL FOR A LUCKY ESCAPE
FROM A RIDING ACCIDENT*

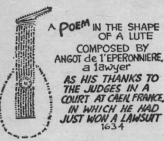

A **POEM** IN THE SHAPE OF A LUTE COMPOSED BY ANGOT de l'EPERONNIERE, a lawyer AS HIS THANKS TO THE JUDGES IN A COURT AT CAEN, FRANCE, IN WHICH HE HAD JUST WON A LAWSUIT 1634

A **ONE-TRACK RAILROAD** CARRIED PASSENGERS FROM RAINCY, FRANCE, TO GAGNY FROM 1868 TO 1870, BUT WAS ABANDONED BECAUSE THE ENGINE'S TWO POWER WHEELS STRADDLED THE TRACK —AND THE PAVEMENT HAD TO BE REPAIRED DAILY

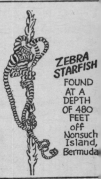

ZEBRA STARFISH FOUND AT A DEPTH OF 480 FEET off Nonsuch Island, Bermuda

ROBINSON CRUSOE II
ALFRED de RODT (1843-1905) a SWISS WHO RENTED THE ISLAND OF JUAN FERNANDEZ, MADE FAMOUS BY ROBINSON CRUSOE, FROM CHILE FOR $1,500 A YEAR WAS ITS GOVERNOR, METEOROLOGIST, JUDGE, REGISTRAR, POLICEMAN, POSTMASTER, TEACHER AND HARBOR MASTER (1877-1905)

THE "HICKSVILLE"
A LOCOMOTIVE BUILT
FOR THE LONG ISLAND
RAILROAD IN 1836
*WAS THE FIRST TO
BE EQUIPPED WITH
A STEAM WHISTLE*

SIR WALTER RALEIGH
(1552 - 1618)
IN THE PERIOD
BETWEEN HIS CONVICTION
FOR HIGH TREASON AND HIS
EXECUTION WAS PROMOTED
TO THE RANK OF GRAND
ADMIRAL AND SENT ON AN
EXPEDITION TO GUIANA

THE TEMPLES OF POLONNARUWA in Ceylon
WERE BUILT WITH BRICKS MADE FROM
A MIXTURE OF SAND, MUD, CLAY, QUARTZ,
BURNT STRAW, CORN OIL AND HONEY, AND THE
BRICKS WERE PUT IN PLACE WITHOUT MORTAR
-YET THEY HAVE ENDURED FOR 600 YEARS
AND THE WALLS STILL HAVE A SWEET SMELL

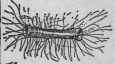

THE INSECT FISHERMEN
THE SILKEN TUBE SPINNERS
-AQUATIC INSECTS-
SPIN DELICATE TUBULAR
NETS OF SILK WHICH
CATCH THE AQUATIC
FAUNA THAT FEED
THEIR LARVA

J. GENE BUTLER and **R. DEAN BUTLER**
of Shelby, N.C.   of Tryon, N.C.
WHO ARE IDENTICAL TWINS,
PLAYING IN THE NATIONAL LEFTHANDED
OPEN GOLF CHAMPIONSHIP
*IN THE SECOND ROUND SCORED
IDENTICAL 83'S*
Hollywood, Florida

**THE FIRST LIFE
INSURANCE POLICY**
WILLIAM GIBBONS
A LONDON SALT MERCHA
HAD HIS LIFE INSURED
FOR $1,894.80 ON JUNE 18,15
*-AND THAT SUM WAS PA
11 MONTHS LATER TO
RICHARD MARTINS,
WHO HAD PAID THE
PREMIUM OF $150,5*

A **JEWELED GOLDEN
CUSPIDOR**
WAS SENT BY KING
MINDON OF BURMA IN
1860 AS A GIFT TO
QUEEN VICTORIA—
*THE QUEEN, IN HER LETTER
OF THANKS, EXPRESSED
ADMIRATION FOR THE
LOVELY "FLOWER VASE"*

THE
"POOR SOLDIER"
of Australia
IS A BIRD
THAT
CONSTANTLY
EMITS A CRY
THAT SOUNDS
LIKE *"POOR
SOLDIER"*

FARM WAGONS
STILL IN USE IN THE SANTA
TERESA NATIONAL PARK, IN URUGUAY,
WERE CONSTRUCTED WITHOUT THE
USE OF A SINGLE NAIL

THE **DESSERT**
SERVED BY KING
JAMES V of Scotland
TO EACH GUEST
AT A BANQUET
*CONSISTED OF A
DEEP DISH FILLED
WITH GOLD PIECES*

THE **CALENDAR CHURCH**
BOSTON CHURCH in England
HAS A STAIRWAY OF **365** STEPS
TO ITS TOWER – A WINDOW FOR EACH
OF THE **52** WEEKS IN THE YEAR
AND **12** PILLARS TO CORRESPOND
WITH THE NUMBER OF MONTHS

**KATHERINE
MAYHEW**
STARTED HER ACTING
CAREER IN GRAFTON, OHIO,
AT THE AGE OF **5**
*AND WAS AN ACTRESS
FOR 77 YEARS*

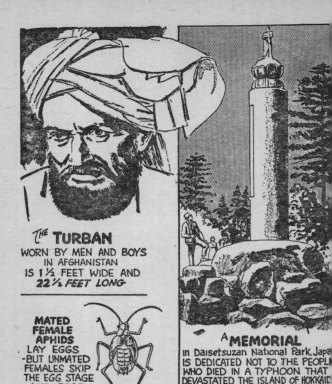

THE TURBAN
WORN BY MEN AND BOYS
IN AFGHANISTAN
IS 1½ FEET WIDE AND
22½ FEET LONG

MATED
FEMALE
APHIDS
LAY EGGS
-BUT UNMATED
FEMALES SKIP
THE EGG STAGE
*AND BEAR
LARVA*

A **MEMORIAL**
In Daisetsuzan National Park, Japan
IS DEDICATED NOT TO THE PEOPLE
WHO DIED IN A TYPHOON THAT
DEVASTATED THE ISLAND OF HOKKAIDO
*-BUT "TO THE SOULS OF
THE TREES THAT DIED "*
1954

THE
**SCHWARZWASSER
RIVER**
near Aue, Saxony,
FORMS THE SHAPE OF A
PERFECT HORSESHOE

THE
STIRRUPS
USED BY
NATIVES
of Marajo
Island,
in the
Amazon
River,
Brazil,
IN RIDING THEIR OXEN
ARE SO NARROW THEY
HOLD ONLY 2 TOES

CLARENCE E. THORPE
of Riverside, Calif.
CAN SIMULTANEOUSLY DRAW ONE CARTOON WITH ONE HAND AND *ANOTHER WITH HIS FOOT*

THE **HORSEMAN**
an island in Norway
SHAPED LIKE A SPIDER ON A BLANKETED HORSE

THE **ACROCOMIA TOTAI PALM**
of Brazil
HAS A TRUNK ARMED BY NATURE WITH SHARP SPINES *TO PREVENT ANIMALS FROM CLIMBING UP TO THE LEAVES*

5 BUTIA PALMS
GROWING FROM *A SINGLE ROOT*
Santa Teresa National Park, Uruguay

CLARA JOHANNSEN of Reval, Estonia, WIDOW OF A SHIP CAPTAIN REPORTED DROWNED IN 1888, CONTINUED TO TURN BACK HER HUSBAND'S BEDCOVERS AND PLACE HIS SLIPPERS BESIDE THE BED NIGHTLY *FOR 22 YEARS*

THE HERB THAT NEVER GETS WET MYRIOPHYLLUM IS AN AQUATIC HERB YET IT IS SURROUNDED BY A CUSHION OF AIR *SO THAT EVEN UNDERWATER IT REMAINS COMPLETELY DRY*

THE CHAPEL of ST. MICHAEL in Challes-les-Eaux, France, *HOLDS SERVICES ONLY ONCE EACH YEAR*

THE FIRST BIRD ARCHAEOPTERYX, WHICH HAS LEFT ITS IMPRESSION IN BEDS OF SLATE, WAS HALF BIRD, HALF REPTILE, COULD ONLY GLIDE AND EXISTED *155,000,000 YEARS AGO*

THE NATIVES WHO NEVER LEAVE THEIR DEATH BEDS

THE KAXINAUA of Brazil WRAP THEIR DEAD IN THE HAMMOCKS WHICH SERVED AS THEIR BEDS —AND BURY THEM UNDER THE EARTHEN FLOORS OF THEIR HOMES

PLANE TREES WHICH LINE THE ROADS OF SOUTHERN FRANCE HAVE THEIR TOPS CUT OFF EACH YEAR —FOR THE LUMBER AND TO ASSURE A BROADER CROWN

THE BANANA HAIRDO

MARRIAGEABLE GIRLS IN Libreville, a region of Gabon, Africa, BRAID THEIR HAIR IN THE SHAPE OF A BUNCH OF BANANAS TO ASSURE A PROSPECTIVE HUSBAND THAT *THEY WILL KEEP HIM WELL FED*

THE CHAPEL OF HELP in Tossa, Spain, *IS USED ON ONLY ONE DAY EACH YEAR*

JOHN WITHERSPOON (1723-1794) of Princeton, N.J., WAS THE ONLY SIGNER OF THE DECLARATION OF INDEPENDENCE *WHO WAS A MEMBER OF THE CLERGY*

THE **MONARCH** WHOSE **UNDERWEAR** BECAME A LIBRARY

KING MINDON WHO RULED BURMA FROM 1853 TO 1878 WORE HIS SILK UNDERGARMENTS ONLY ONCE - *BUT IT WAS FORBIDDEN TO DESTROY THEM OR TO GIVE THEM TO ANYONE ELSE TO WEAR* THEY WERE CUT INTO STRIPS AND BOUND INTO BOOKS ON WHICH THE BURMESE SCRIPTURES WERE INSCRIBED

POSTAGE STAMP of the Tonga Islands, in the Pacific, -A REPRODUCTION OF THE GEOGRAPHICAL OUTLINE OF THE KINGDOM

A NEST SHAPED LIKE A STAR IS BUILT BY THE TILAPIA FISH OF THE CONGO TO ASSURE ITS EGGS BETTER VENTILATION BY THE CURRENTS AT THE BOTTOM OF THE RIVER

THE CHURCH OF SAN ADRIAN Mount Aizkorri, Spain, IS CONSTRUCTED INSIDE A CAVE

PIERRE-CHARLES DEBRAY

AS PUNISHMENT FOR FIRING AT RUSSIAN TROOPS IN PARIS, FRANCE, IN 1814, WAS PINNED TO THE WALL OF A STABLE BY A LANCE THRUST THROUGH HIS BODY —YET HE RECOVERED AND LIVED FOR ANOTHER 30 YEARS
FOR THE REMAINDER OF HIS LIFE THE ONLY FOOD HE COULD DIGEST WAS MILK

YOUNG MEN of the Yoruba Tribe, Africa, PROPOSE BY SENDING THE GIRL 6 COWRIE SHELLS BECAUSE THE YORUBA WORD FOR 6 ALSO MEANS: "I AM ATTRACTED TO YOU." THE GIRL USUALLY SENDS BACK A NECKLACE OF 8 SHELLS—BECAUSE THE YORUBA WORD FOR 8 ALSO MEANS: "OK"

PYRAMID FORMED OF DOMINOES, CHECKERS AND CHESS PIECES —BALANCED ON A SINGLE DOMINO

DRUMS

USED BY THE
ANCIENT ROMANS WERE
COVERED WITH WOLF
SKINS IN THE BELIEF
THEY WOULD PRODUCE
THE GREATEST SOUND
-*BECAUSE THE LOUDEST
NOISE IN THE
FORESTS WAS THE
HOWLING OF WOLVES*

CHURCHES
in England in
the 14th and
15th centuries
HAD NO SEATS
AND WORSHIPERS
SAT ON THE FLOOR

WRAP
IT UP!

A **HUGE WHITE WHALE**
CAUGHT OFF
Newfoundland in 1878
WAS SHIPPED TO
London, England,
*WRAPPED IN
SEAWEED IN A
PACKING CASE*
IT COMPLETED
THE 5-WEEK
VOYAGE IN
EXCELLENT
CONDITION

*ROAD
SIGN*
in
Queen Elizabeth
National Park
Uganda, Africa

ELEPHANTS
HAVE RIGHT
OF WAY

THE CATERPILLAR of the Lycaenida butterfly *ALWAYS FORMS A PARTNERSHIP WITH AN ANT*

THE CATERPILLAR RELEASES A SUGARY LIQUID WHICH FEEDS THE ANT - AND THE ANT PRODUCES A HONEY THAT IS EATEN BY THE CATERPILLAR

THE **"BIRDCAGE"** REMAINS WHEN THE BLOOMS FADE ON THE DUNE PRIMROSE, A FLOWER FOUND IN THE COLORADO DESERT

ILDEFONSO GOMEZ (1731-1858) WAS A SPANISH SOLDIER UNTIL HE WAS 77 YEARS OF AGE, SUFFERED 28 WOUNDS IN BATTLE, MARRIED AT THE AGE OF 84; AND *LIVED TO THE AGE OF 127*

THE **"U.S.S. MAINE"** CREATED AS A REPLICA OF THE BATTLESHIP, EVEN TO SIZE, BY JOHN LAIDLAW, A SCOTTISH GARDENER, *ENTIRELY FROM FLOWERS* IT WAS CREATED IN THE YARDS OF THE MICHIGAN CENTRAL RAILWAY, IN YPSILANTI, MICHIGAN

MESSAGES SENT TO FRIENDS BY ENRICO TAZZOLI, ITALIAN PATRIOT HELD PRISONER BY THE AUSTRIANS, *WERE WRITTEN ON HANDKERCHIEFS IN HIS OWN BLOOD* (1852.)

THE GREAT CANOPY OVER **St. PETER'S TOMB**-in Rome- IS SUPPORTED BY 4 BRONZE PILLARS EACH OF WHICH WEIGHS EXACTLY 27,948 POUNDS BUILDER GIANLORENZO BERNINI PLEDGED HIS PERSONAL WEALTH AS A GUARANTEE *THAT THE COLUMNS WOULD NOT VARY IN·WEIGHT BY EVEN AN OUNCE*

PROFESSOR ERNST LUDWIG NEBEL (1772-1854) who taught medicine at the University of Giessen, Germany, FOR 56 YEARS, WAS SO AVERSE TO WEARING A CLEAN SHIRT NEXT TO HIS SKIN THAT HE OFTEN DONNED A CLEAN SHIRT OVER *AS MANY AS 5 DIRTY SHIRTS*

SPADE FISH *CHANGE COLOR INSTANTLY FROM BLACK TO WHITE*

THE **OFFICE** OF WALTER MEDICIS of Syracuse, N.Y., IN THE PURCHASING DEPARTMENT OF SYRACUSE UNIVERSITY, IS LOCATED IN THE BUILDING THAT FORMERLY SERVED AS SYRACUSE HOSPITAL -AT THE EXACT SPOT WHERE HIS FATHER, JOSEPH G. MEDICIS. SR., RECOVERED FROM WORLD WAR I WOUNDS 49 YEARS AGO

THE MAN WHO WAS CONSIDERED AS DANGEROUS AS 3 BATTLESHIPS!

THOMAS MUIR (1765-1798) A SCOTTISH LAWYER WHO WAS SENTENCED TO 14 YEARS DEPORTATION, BUT ESCAPED FROM AUSTRALIA, WAS CONSIDERED SO IMPORTANT A PRISONER THAT THE BRITISH GOVERNMENT *OFFERED THE KING OF SPAIN 3 WARSHIPS FOR HIS CUSTODY* MUIR HAD BEEN CONVICTED OF RECITING THOMAS PAINE'S "THE RIGHTS OF MAN"

THE **MEMORIAL** TO A BASHFUL **PHILANTHROPIST** Lyon, France A STATUE OF JEAN KLEBERG WHO PROVIDED DOWRIES FOR SCORES OF INDIGENT BRIDES STANDS IN A CAVE IN WHICH KLEBERG USED TO FIND REFUGE *TO ESCAPE THE GRATITUDE OF HIS BENEFICIARIES*

THE TEMPLE OF THE BELL OF A THOUSAND AGES at Yanyang, China, TO MAKE CERTAIN ITS BELL WILL LAST A HUNDRED THOUSAND YEARS RINGS IT ONLY *ONCE EACH CENTURY*

THE PARSEES of India ADHERENTS OF THE ANCIENT PERSIAN RELIGION *WEAR HATS SHAPED LIKE THE HOOF OF A COW*

THE GREAT ROCKING STONE near Waidhausen, Austria, *CAN ACTUALLY BE ROCKED TO AND FRO*

THE ISLAND OF PIC in Cambodia BEARS A REMARKABLE RESEMBLANCE *TO A PREHISTORIC MONSTER*

A MIRAGE IN THE FORM OF 3 SUNS, SURROUNDED BY 2 CRESCENTS, VISIBLE TO THOUSANDS IN THE SKY OVER JAFFA, PALESTINE, ON JANUARY 26, 1567

WILLIAM PITT (1759-1806) THE CELEBRATED ENGLISH STATESMAN COMPLETED EACH DINNER BY *GULPING DOWN 2 BOTTLES OF PORT WINE*

THE **JAM JAR LIFEBOAT** INVENTED IN 1831 BY A MAN NAMED BATEMAN WHO INSISTED IT WAS UNSINKABLE *SANK THE FIRST TIME IT WAS TESTED*

SINGLE GIRLS of the Fiji Islands ADVERTISED THEY WERE SEEKING A HUSBAND BY *WEARING THEIR HAIR IN BRAIDS OVER ONE SHOULDER*

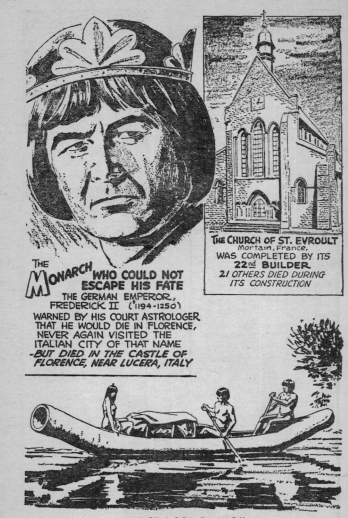

THE CHURCH OF ST. EVROULT
Mortain, France,
WAS COMPLETED BY ITS
22nd BUILDER
*21 OTHERS DIED DURING
ITS CONSTRUCTION*

THE MONARCH WHO COULD NOT ESCAPE HIS FATE

THE GERMAN EMPEROR,
FREDERICK II ('1194-1250)
WARNED BY HIS COURT ASTROLOGER
THAT HE WOULD DIE IN FLORENCE,
NEVER AGAIN VISITED THE
ITALIAN CITY OF THAT NAME
*-BUT DIED IN THE CASTLE OF
FLORENCE, NEAR LUCERA, ITALY*

THE "DONUT BOATS"
CARIPUNA INDIANS of the state of Amazonas, Brazil, IN HOLLOWING-
OUT THEIR DUGOUT CANOES, LEAVE AT EITHER END OF THE CRAFT THE FULL
TRUNK OF THE ORIGINAL TREE -WITH A HOLE BURNED THROUGH THE CENTER

"THE BRAVEST" ROMAN OF THEM ALL

Caius Silius

A CITIZEN OF ANCIENT ROME, MARRIED EMPRESS MESSALINA *WHEN SHE WAS STILL THE WIFE OF EMPEROR CLAUDIUS*— FRIENDS POINTED OUT TO THE EMPEROR THAT THE COUPLE WOULD NEVER HAVE DARED TO WED IF THEY HAD NOT PLANNED TO ASSASSINATE HIM— *SO HE HAD THEM BOTH EXECUTED* (48 A.D.)

THE TEMPLE
NATURAL STONE FORMATION OVERLOOKING THE COLORADO RIVER, in Nev.

THE BAPTISMAL FONT
OF THE CHURCH OF ALCALÁ de HENARES, in Spain, USED FOR THE BAPTISM OF MIGUEL DE CERVANTES, THE AUTHOR OF "DON QUIXOTE," SMASHED TO BITS DURING THE CIVIL WAR OF 1936—*WAS REBUILT FROM THE FRAGMENTS*

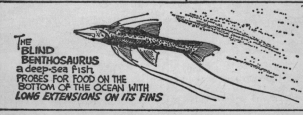

THE BLIND BENTHOSAURUS
a deep-sea fish PROBES FOR FOOD ON THE BOTTOM OF THE OCEAN WITH *LONG EXTENSIONS ON ITS FINS*

THE BELFRY NATURAL STONE FORMATION Val Montanaia, Italy

HALF A HIPPIE

AN ABORIGINE of Australia DEMONSTRATES DISTINCTION AND HIGH RANK BY SHAVING ONLY HALF OF HIS FACE

THE OFFICIAL SEAL of Aussig, Czechoslovakia, READS: "HE WHO GIVES ALL HIS MONEY TO HIS CHILDREN, THEN SUFFERS WANT, LET ME SLAY HIM WITH MY CLUB"

THE SIJU TREE IS WORSHIPED BY the Kachari Tribe of India AS THE GOD WHO GUARDS EACH FAMILY'S PROSPERITY AND HONOR

JAN GREVE JAILED IN AMSTERDAM IN 1619 FOR PREACHING WITHOUT A LICENSE AND KEPT IN A PITCH BLACK CELL FOR 1½ YEARS *WROTE HIS FAMOUS BOOK "TRIBUNAL REFORMATUM" IN TOTAL DARKNESS*

THE **GRANDFATHER'S CLOCK** IN THE COLEMAN HOUSE Nantucket, STOPPED ONLY ONCE IN 115 YEARS -AND THAT WAS ON THE DAY AN EARTHQUAKE SHOOK LISBON, PORTUGAL **3,000 MILES AWAY** Nov.1,1755

BEEHIVES in France ARE COVERED WITH BLACK CREPE BY PEASANTS AFTER A DEATH IN THE OWNER'S FAMILY IN THE BELIEF THAT OTHERWISE THE BEES *WOULD FLY AWAY AND NEVER RETURN*

THE **SEA CUCUMBER** HAS NEITHER A HEAD NOR EYES *AND HURLS ITS ENTRAILS AT AN ENEMY*

A **MARKER** SHARED BY HUNGARY, AUSTRIA AND YUGOSLAVIA

THE SOLDIER WHOSE LIFE WAS SAVED BY SHRAPNEL

HENRY TORRÈS a celebrated French attorney HIT BY GERMAN SHRAPNEL IN WORLD WAR I SUSTAINED 26 WOUNDS—

ONE FRAGMENT ENTERED HIS LUNGS AND RESTRICTED HIS BREATHING —WHICH SAVED HIS LIFE DURING A GERMAN GAS ATTACK

THE PROCESSIONARY CATERPILLARS

ALWAYS TRAVEL IN CHAIN FORMATION AND DURING PERIODS OF REST THE CHAIN CLOSES *TO FORM A TIGHT CIRCLE*

THE SKOMER VOLE

a rodent, IS FOUND NOWHERE IN THE WORLD *EXCEPT ON SKOMER ISLAND- IN PEMBROKESHIRE, WALES*

THE PERFECTIONIST
JOHN GARLAND Justice of the Peace of Barrington, N.H., in 1776 SENT HIS SON, FRANK, OUT TO FIND A PROPER "BACKLOG" FOR HIS FIREPLACE, WARNING HIM: *"DON'T RETURN UNTIL YOU FIND A LOG OF THE PROPER SIZE."* **FRANK CAME BACK WITH THE LOG 9 YEARS LATER**

THE CHURCH of the HOLY SPIRIT in Heidelberg, Germany, SINCE 1487 HAS PERMITTED OPERATION OF STORES BETWEEN ITS OUTER PILLARS

ERNEST BRAUNINGER of Correctionville, Iowa, CAN CHIN HIMSELF WITH 2 FINGERS WITH 25 POUNDS OF BRICKS ROPED TO HIS BACK AT THE AGE of 71

GEORGES CLEMENCEAU (1841-1929) WHEN REFRESHMENTS WERE BEING SERVED WAS ASKED BY PRESIDENT FALLIÈRES, OF FRANCE, IN 1906, "WHAT WILL YOU TAKE?"

MISUNDERSTANDING THE QUESTION, CLEMENCEAU REPLIED, "I'LL TAKE THE MINISTRY OF THE INTERIOR." HE GOT THE JOB

THE MEADOW A CHURCH BUILT ON A MEADOW AT THE FOOT OF MOUNT HOHEN BLEICK, NEAR STEINGADEN, GERMANY, *WAS CONSTRUCTED IN THE SHAPE OF THE 5,300-FT. MOUNTAIN*

HANS SACHS

1494-1576
THE GERMAN
POET
WROTE
196 PLAYS
313 SHORT
STORIES
307 LONG
POEMS
59 FABLES
AND 5,173
*MINSTREL
ACTS*

THE GRAVE of HENRY WOOLDRIDGE, in Maplewood Cemetery, Mayfield, Ky. IS ADORNED BY 16 STATUES - *DEPICTING WOOLDRIDGE MEMBERS OF HIS FAMILY, AND HIS HORSE, 2 DOGS, A FOX AND A DEER*

THE
COMMUNITY
THAT COULD NOT BE COWED

PITSCHEN, a town in Poland founded in the 13th century, WAS DESTROYED BY FIRE 8 TIMES AND BY ENEMY INVASIONS 12 TIMES -YET IT WAS REBUILT EACH TIME

FELICE de ROVIGNY
(1812 -1907)
JILTED IN LOVE AT THE AGE OF 20 *NEVER AGAIN LEFT HER APARTMENT UNTIL HER DEATH 75 YEARS LATER*
Paris, France

THOMAS MAY
(1595-1650) the English poet WAS CHOKED TO DEATH BY THE *'RIBBONS OF HIS NIGHTCAP'*

THE
SEA
PARROT of the Arctic
CAN DIVE TO A DEPTH OF 200 FEET

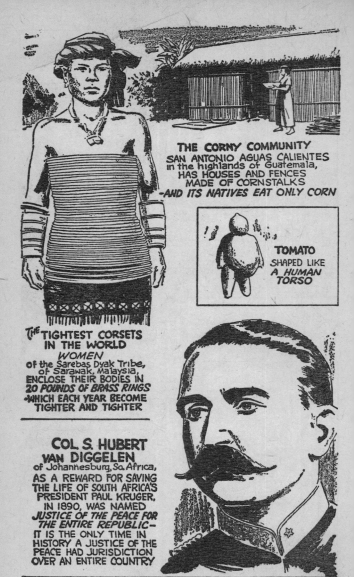

THE CORNY COMMUNITY
SAN ANTONIO AGUAS CALIENTES
in the highlands of Guatemala,
HAS HOUSES AND FENCES
MADE OF CORNSTALKS
-AND ITS NATIVES EAT ONLY CORN

TOMATO
SHAPED LIKE
*A HUMAN
TORSO*

**THE TIGHTEST CORSETS
IN THE WORLD**
WOMEN
Of the Sarebas Dyak Tribe,
of Sarawak, Malaysia,
ENCLOSE THEIR BODIES IN
20 POUNDS OF BRASS RINGS
-WHICH EACH YEAR BECOME
TIGHTER AND TIGHTER

**COL. S. HUBERT
VAN DIGGELEN**
of Johannesburg, So. Africa,
AS A REWARD FOR SAVING
THE LIFE OF SOUTH AFRICA'S
PRESIDENT PAUL KRUGER,
IN 1890, WAS NAMED
*JUSTICE OF THE PEACE FOR
THE ENTIRE REPUBLIC—*
IT IS THE ONLY TIME IN
HISTORY A JUSTICE OF THE
PEACE HAD JURISDICTION
OVER AN ENTIRE COUNTRY

ANCIENT CHINESE COIN
SHAPED LIKE A FISH

MEMORIAL TO AN IDLE BOAST
THE TOWER OF VICTORY in Yunnan-Fu, China, 150 FEET HIGH, WAS BUILT BY VICEROY TSEN YU YING IN 1874 *IN ANTICIPATION OF A VICTORY HE EXPECTED TO WIN OVER THE TONKINESE* HE WAS DEFEATED BUT THE TOWER STILL STANDS

THE SECOND EARL OF ROCHESTER
(1647-1680) English poet WAS INTOXICATED CONSTANTLY *FOR 5 YEARS*

THE FIGUREHEAD
OF THE S.S. EMPRESS OF JAPAN ERECTED IN STANLEY PARK, VANCOUVER, B.C., AS A *MEMORIAL TO THE VESSEL*

PILATE'S HOUSE in Oberammergau, Germany, SCENE OF THE FAMOUS PASSION PLAYS, IS A GIGANTIC OPTICAL ILLUSION ALL THE "PROJECTIONS" ON THE HOUSE *ACTUALLY ARE PAINTED ON A FLAT FACADE*

PEASANTS of Forez, France, DEMONSTRATED THEIR OPPOSITION TO THE REVOLUTION BY SHAVING THEIR HEADS, LEAVING 2 LOCKS OF HAIR HANGING IN FRONT OF THEIR EARS -A REPLICA OF THE HAIRCUT OF *THOSE CONDEMNED TO THE GUILLOTINE*

3 CAMELS WERE TAUGHT BY ANIMAL TRAINER ELLIOTT HUMPHREY *TO WALK BACKWARDS - IN STEP -* HUMPHREY HAD BEEN TOLD NO CAMEL COULD BE TAUGHT TO BACK UP

THE BIZARRE BRIDAL BARTERS OF THE BAIRAGIS

NATIVES in the area of Gaur, India, STAGE A MARRIAGE MARKET ONCE EACH YEAR WITH THE SINGLE GIRLS CONCEALED IN BULKY COVERINGS AND THE PROSPECTIVE *GROOMS PAYING 80¢ EACH TO PICK A BRIDE AT RANDOM—* AFTER VIEWING HIS BRIDE THE MAN CAN TURN HER BACK AND PAY ANOTHER 80¢ FOR A SECOND CHOICE—BUT THE THIRD SELECTION IS ALWAYS FINAL

QUEEN LOUISE, wife of KING HENRY III, WHO RULED FRANCE FROM 1574 TO 1589 *PERMITTED NO ONE BUT HER HUSBAND TO DRESS HER OR COMB HER HAIR*

LEATHER BRIDLES ARE STILL CUT FROM COWHIDES IN SPIRALS BY THE BASQUES OF SPAIN *—A METHOD ORIGINATED BY THEIR CAVEMEN ANCESTORS*

THE EQUIBUS
INVENTED IN BOSTON, MASS., IN 1878
HAD DRIVER, PASSENGERS —AND HORSE—
ALL INSIDE THE CARRIAGE

ARCHIBALD CAMPBELL
A SCHOOLTEACHER
near Fredericksburg, Va.,
TAUGHT 3 FUTURE
PRESIDENTS OF THE
UNITED STATES —
GEORGE WASHINGTON
JAMES MADISON
AND JAMES MONROE

A **POLITICIAN WHO SAID HE WOULDN'T
SERVE —AND REALLY MEANT IT!**
JOSSE GOETHALS
ELECTED A COUNCILMAN IN GHENT,
FLANDERS, IN 1526, REFUSED TO
ACCEPT THE OFFICE ALTHOUGH HIS
DECISION BY LAW MEANT THE
LOPPING OFF OF BOTH HIS EARS

THE **NORTH
AFRICAN
MANE SHEEP,**
FOUND
ONLY IN THE
DESERT,
*DRINKS
WATER
ONLY
ONCE
EVERY
6 DAYS*

A **PATH** ON THE CAMPUS OF CENTRAL COLLEGE, in Pella, Iowa, WAS CONSTRUCTED IN THE SHAPE OF THE LETTER "S" IN 1878 AS A MEMORIAL TO *DR. EMANUEL H. SCARFF,* A POPULAR INSTRUCTOR AT THE SCHOOL FOR 24 YEARS

THE **11th DUKE of NORFOLK** (1746-1815) THE HIGHEST RANKING DUKE IN ENGLAND *NEVER WASHED OR BATHED*

THE **STRANGEST OPEN SESAME IN NATURE** THE HERRING GULL HAS A BLACK MARK ON ITS BEAK AND ITS YOUNG CAN INDUCE THEIR MOTHER TO REGURGITATE A FISH AS THEIR FOOD ONLY *BY TAPPING THAT SPOT*

A **BRONZE VASE** FOUND IN A subterranean temple in Paestum, Italy, HAD BEEN BURIED 2,600 YEARS EARLIER -YET IT WAS *STILL HALF FULL OF HONEY*

THE "HORN" MOTH
(Holocerina angulata)
of Africa
HAS ROLLED WINGS
THAT LOOK LIKE THE
BELL OF A TRUMPET

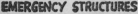

EMERGENCY STRUCTURES
ERECTED IN HAMBURG, GERMANY, IN
1842, AS TEMPORARY HOMES AFTER
THE CITY WAS DESTROYED
BY A GREAT FIRE, ARE STILL
IN USE AS DWELLINGS
126 YEARS LATER

THE **PANCHEN LAMA**
PUPPET RULER OF TIBET
WHOSE PEOPLE WORSHIP HIM
*IS THE ONLY COMMUNIST IN THE
WORLD WHO DOUBLES AS A "GOD"*

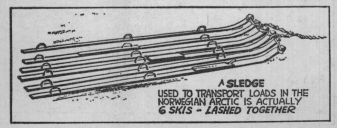

A SLEDGE
USED TO TRANSPORT LOADS IN THE
NORWEGIAN ARCTIC IS ACTUALLY
6 SKIS - LASHED TOGETHER

THE ANCIENT PERSIANS CUT DOWN ENEMY SOLDIERS BY ATTACHING SHARP SICKLES TO THE WHEELS AND THE SHAFTS OF THEIR CHARIOTS

THE WHITE LEAF CROSS
Near Princes Risborough, England
IT WAS CUT INTO THE CHALK OF THE HILL BY KING EDWARD THE ELDER IN **910** —AND HAS BEEN MAINTAINED AS A LANDMARK FOR TRAVELERS FOR 1058 YEARS

THE FEMALE WATERBUG of MADAGASCAR DEPOSITS HER EGGS ON THE WINGS OF THE MALE WHOSE WINGS ARE THUS SEALED SO HE *CANNOT FLY AWAY UNTIL THE YOUNG ARE HATCHED*

A STERLET
A TYPE OF FISH FROM WHICH ISINGLASS IS OBTAINED, SURVIVED IN THE BRIGHTON AQUARIUM, ENGLAND, *FOR 38 YEARS*

MODEL PAINTER

CRISTOFANO ALLORI (1577-1619) the Italian painter, CONVINCED THAT NO MODEL COULD FOLLOW HIS EXACTING INSTRUCTIONS *ALWAYS POSED FOR HIS OWN PICTURES*

A FRIEND SKETCHED HIM IN EACH POSE AND THEN ALLORI COMPLETED THE PAINTING

AMY JOHNSON

WHO FLEW SOLO FROM ENGLAND TO AUSTRALIA IN 1930 IN AN OPEN-COCKPIT PLANE WAS UNABLE TO SELL HER STORY BEFORE THE FLIGHT FOR $125 — AFTER SHE REACHED AUSTRALIA MISS JOHNSON RECEIVED $50,000 FOR THE STORY

THE GREAT CLOCK
ON THE OLD CITY HALL of Prague, Czechoslovakia, HAS BEEN RUNNING WITHOUT PAUSE SINCE 1490 – *ITS PERPETUAL CALENDAR AND ANIMATED FIGURES BEING CONSIDERED A WONDER OF THE AGES* – YET IT HAS NOT ONCE SHOWN THE CORRECT TIME IN 478 YEARS

THE **5th LORD ELIBANK** (1703-1778) WAS APPOINTED A CAPTAIN IN A SCOTTISH REGIMENT – WITH THE SALARY OF HIS RANK AND 2 SERVANTS · AT *THE AGE OF 3*

PHAETHON AETHEREUS of FIJI IS CONSIDERED SO SACRED A BIRD THAT IT IS FORBIDDEN FOR *A HUMAN EVEN TO TOUCH IT*

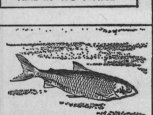

THE **GWYNIAD** a fish in Bala Lake, Wales, *IS FOUND NOWHERE ELSE IN THE WORLD*

AN **ANCIENT ROMAN CHARIOT** MADE OF MARBLE – WAS USED IN THE CHURCH OF ST. MARK, in Rome, AS A BISHOP'S CHAIR FOR *350 YEARS*

NATIVES of the Waiwai Tribe ON THE BORDER BETWEEN BRAZIL AND BRITISH GUIANA WEAR AN ARTIFICIAL MOUSTACHE - MADE BY PIERCING THEIR NOSE WITH LONG FEATHERS

A **POSTAGE STAMP** IN THE SHAPE OF A HEART WAS ISSUED BY THE KINGDOM OF THE TONGA ISLANDS IN THE PACIFIC *FOR USE ON LOVE LETTERS*

THE **OLD WOODEN BRIDGE** WHICH HAD SPANNED Kangaroo Valley, in New South Wales, Australia, FOR NEARLY 100 YEARS, WAS REPLACED BY A MODERN SUSPENSION BRIDGE ON FEB. 8, 1898 – AND A FLOOD WASHED AWAY THE *OLD BRIDGE ONLY 6 DAYS LATER*

BAMBOO BRIDGES built by natives of the Kacha Naga Tribe of Assam SHOW AN AMAZING KNOWLEDGE OF ENGINEERING - THE THIN BAMBOO STICKS BEING TRUSSED AND COUNTERWEIGHTED TO FORM A TRUE CANTILEVER SPAN

THE S.S. SHUTONG

CAUGHT IN THE GODDESS OF MERCY RAPIDS OF THE YANGTZE GORGE, IN CHINA, WAS TOSSED ONTO A REEF 30 FEET ABOVE THE WATER AND RESTED THERE FOR 40 DAYS -YET WHEN REFLOATED IT WAS FOUND TO BE COMPLETELY UNDAMAGED
(1908)

THE BARRACUDA

WHEN IT IS ASLEEP DISPLAYS DARK STRIPES ON ITS BODY - *BUT THEY ALWAYS DISAPPEAR WHEN IT IS AWAKE*

THE NEW ZEALAND FANTAIL

CAMOUFLAGES ITS NEST BY GIVING IT A STREAMER OF MOSS AND WOOL SO *PREDATORS WILL THINK IT IS A PLANT*

NATIVES

OF THE RIES REGION OF Germany REVEAL THEIR RELIGIOUS AFFILIATION EACH MARKET DAY *BY THE EPAULETS ON THEIR COSTUMES*

A HOLLOW TREE
near Ahmedabad, India,
WHICH FOR YEARS WAS THE
HOME OF AN INDIAN HERMIT

A **PACK** OF
CIGARETS
CREATED BY THE
RUSSIAN SECRET
POLICE IN 1954
*ACTUALLY WAS
A GUN*
IT WAS TO BE USED
IN AN ATTEMPTED
MURDER IN
FRANKFURT AM
MAIN, GERMANY

AN **OX** RAISED BY
JOB TYLER, OF
QUAKER NECK, N.J., IN 1818
*REACHED A WEIGHT
OF 2,165 POUNDS*

THE
WHITE RAT
IS ACTUALLY
A GOLDFISH

THE TINY HAND
OF FABULOUSLY BEAUTIFUL YANG KUEI FEI
-FAVORITE OF CHINESE EMPEROR MING HUANG-
OUTLINED BY A SCULPTOR ON A STONE
AT THE SIAN-FU PALACE SITE, BECAME
A DEEP HOLLOW IN THE HARD STONE
*AS THOUSANDS OF WOMEN
MEASURED THEIR HANDS AGAINST YANG'S
OVER A PERIOD OF 1,200 YEARS*

THE **SPOONBILL** HAS THE EQUIVALENT OF A FINGERNAIL ON *THE TIP OF ITS TONGUE*

MARY ANN LLOYD of Dymock, England, GAVE A TEA FOR HER FRIEND, MRS. HELEN TASKER, WHEN THE GUEST OF HONOR WAS 100 *AND THE HOSTESS WAS* **103**

THE **DUCHESS d'UZÈS** (1847-1933) *WEALTHIEST WIDOW IN FRANCE WORE MOURNING DAILY FOR THE LAST 55 YEARS OF HER LIFE* BUT SHE WAS THE FIRST FRENCH-WOMAN TO DRIVE A CAR AND BECAME A FAMED HUNTRESS WHO KILLED **2,000** STAGS

THE **REV. JOHN KIRBY**
VICAR OF MAYFIELD, ENGLAND,
FROM 1780 TO 1810,
WAS THE FATHER, GRANDFATHER
AND GREAT-GRANDFATHER OF
VICARS OF MAYFIELD — *A POST
FILLED BY THE FAMILY
FOR 132 YEARS*

**KNIGHT
LIGHTS**
KNIGHTS
in
medieval times
WHEN ENGAGING
IN BATTLES
AFTER DARK
*CARRIED
LIGHTED
LANTERNS
AFFIXED
TO THEIR
SADDLES*

THE NAVEL STONE
THE REGISTRY OF ROYAL BIRTHS
ON KAUAI, HAWAII, WAS A ROCK
IN WHICH A CAVITY WAS CHISELED
TO HOLD THE BIRTH RECORD OF
EACH ROYAL BABY AND
ITS UMBILICAL CORD

THE BARON D'ESPAGNAC
(1713 - 1783)
FOR THE LAST 19 YEARS OF HIS LIFE ALWAYS DINED WITH 3 PEOPLE —*ONE OF WHOM HAD TO BE FROM HIS NATIVE TOWN OF BRIVES,* ANOTHER FROM BRESSE, WHERE HE WAS A MILITARY COMMANDER, AND THE THIRD FROM "*LES INVALIDES*" – THE VETERANS' HOME IN PARIS OF WHICH HE HAD BECOME THE GOVERNOR

GERMAIN NOUVEAU
(1851-1920) FRENCH POET, COLLEGE PROFESSOR AND PAINTER SUDDENLY GAVE UP THOSE CAREERS AT THE AGE OF 34 *TO BECOME A TRAMP* – BEGGING FOR FOOD AND FINALLY DYING IN A HOVEL

A **CAVE** near Dambulla, India, IN WHICH THERE ARE 5 TEMPLES **CONSTRUCTED 700 YEARS AGO**

RUSSIAN ROULETTE WITH A CANOE

THE WAIMANGU GEYSER of New Zealand IS THE WORLD'S LARGEST GEYSER, YET ALF WARBRICK AND JOHN BUCKERIDGE ONCE PADDLED A CANOE ON IT FOR 12 MINUTES

ALTHOUGH AT INTERVALS THE GEYSER HURLS ROCKS, MUD AND WATER 1,000 FEET INTO THE AIR -Aug. 10, 1903

THE **KHMER KINGS** of Cambodia, IN ANCIENT TIMES WERE TRANSPORTED IN 2-WHEELED CARTS OF GOLD - PULLED BY SERVANTS WHO WORE HEADDRESSES IN THE SHAPE OF HORSES' HEADS

JACK OF ALL TRADES

JAMES CAMERON
English missionary to Madagascar

WAS ALSO SKILLED AS A PRINTER
ENGINEER
CHEMIST
GLASSMAKER
POTTER
GEOGRAPHER
ASTRONOMER
PHOTOGRAPHER
SURVEYOR
ARCHITECT
MASON AND
BRICKMAKER

THE REVERSIBLE RIVER

The ARAL RIVER in Sind, Pakistan, FOR 6 MONTHS OF EACH YEAR FLOWS FROM THE INDUS RIVER TO LAKE MANCHHAR BUT THE REST OF THE TIME *IT FLOWS FROM THE LAKE BACK TO THE RIVER*

GIBBAEUM ALBUM a South African plant, LOOKS EXACTLY LIKE THE WHITE QUARTZ PEBBLES AMONG WHICH IT ALWAYS GROWS

HUGE KNOTS adorn the Gate of Vila Viçosa, Portugal — A GRAPHIC REMINDER THAT THE BUILDER *WAS FETTERED DAY AND NIGHT AS A CAPTIVE OF THE BARBARY PIRATES*

FRANCESCO BARBIERI (1590-1666) *ONE OF THE LEADING PAINTERS OF HIS TIME* NEVER SET A PRICE ON HIS WORKS OF ART — ACCEPTING WHATEVER A CUSTOMER OFFERED HIM

JEAN CHARCOT (1867-1936)
the French explorer
ON HIS EXPEDITION TO THE
ANTARCTIC IN 1908
HARDENED HIS BODY TO
WITHSTAND THE INTENSE COLD
BY WALKING THE DECK OF
HIS SHIP IN TEMPERATURES
30° BELOW ZERO
-DRESSED ONLY IN THIN
LINEN PAJAMAS

THE **CHATEAU** of **LA TOUR d' AIGUES**
in France
WAS BUILT BY BARON BOULIER
TO WIN THE LOVE OF
QUEEN MARGUERITE de VALOIS
-BUT SHE NEVER EVEN SPARED
THE TIME TO LOOK AT IT

A **7-POUND WILD GOOSE**
MISSED BY 6 SHOTS FIRED BY
WILLIAM BATTLE AND WAYNE LEE
WHEN IT FLEW ONLY 20 FEET
ABOVE THEIR BLIND -*DIED
OF FRIGHT* (Dunnville, Ont.)

AN **ANGEL**
DEPICTED ON THE CEILING
OF KRANICHSTEIN CASTLE,
near Darmstadt, Germany,
*TURNS TO POINT THE
DIRECTION OF THE
PREVAILING WINDS
OUTSIDE THE
CASTLE*

THE **AMAZING BARN OF LEIXLIP**
Ireland
IT IS 73 FEET HIGH, WITH AN
OUTSIDE CIRCULAR STAIRWAY
OF 94 STEPS, AND WAS BUILT
DURING THE FAMINE OF 1742
*TO PROVIDE EMPLOYMENT
FOR THE NEEDY*

AMRA TARAFA (544-570)
celebrated Arab poet
WAS BURIED ALIVE BY
ORDER OF PRINCE AMRU
BEN HIND BECAUSE
THE *PRINCE DISLIKED
A 2-LINE EPIGRAM
TARAFA WROTE*

THE **CASTLES OF ICHANG GORGE**, China
NATURAL ROCK FORMATIONS

THE **WHELK**
LAYS 500 EGGS AT A
TIME, BUT NOT MORE THAN
4 EVER SURVIVE —
*THE OTHERS DEVOUR
EACH OTHER*

MRS. LILLIAN GANDY of Corbin City, N.J., WAS ELECTED TO HER 12th 4-YEAR-TERM AS TAX COLLECTOR AT THE AGE OF 93

THE SATOL A "MOUSETRAP" STILL USED BY BASQUE SHEPHERDS CONSISTS OF A BOARD AND A HEAVY STONE -BALANCED SO THE MOUSE IS CRUSHED WHEN IT GOES UNDER IT FOR THE BAIT

THE TUBA PLANT of Borneo HAS A ROOT SO POISONOUS THAT EATING IT PROVES FATAL TO EVERY MAMMAL -EXCEPT THE PORCUPINE AND THE RHINOCEROS

THE TREE TEMPLE OF BALI A SHRINE CONSTRUCTED HIGH AMONG THE AERIAL ROOTS OF A SACRED FIG TREE

THE PILLARS SUPPORTING THE PORCHES OF HUTS BUILT IN THE SUDAN, AFRICA, BY DINKA TRIBESMEN ARE LIVE TREES —SO BIRDS WILL NEST IN THEM AND CHEER UP THE OCCUPANTS WITH THEIR SONG—

THE FAVORITE SPORT of King Louis XI of France (1423-1483) WAS WATCHING RATS FIGHT

A KIWI BIRD COVERING AN AREA OF 1¼ ACRES (Bulford, England) WAS CARVED IN THE CHALK CLIFF BY NEW ZEALAND SOLDIERS

THE BELFRY
OF ST. JOHN'S CHURCH,
in Kronberg, Germany,
*WAS BUILT 400 YEARS
BEFORE THE REST OF
THE EDIFICE*
THE BELFRY ORIGINALLY
SERVED AS A WATCH TOWER
ON THE CITY WALL

A **PORTRAIT** of **MARTHA WASHINGTON**
WAS WORN AROUND HIS NECK
BY GEORGE WASHINGTON
*EVERY MOMENT OF EVERY DAY
FOR 40 YEARS*
IT WAS REMOVED ONLY AFTER HIS DEATH

**GOLD
MEDAL**
PRESENTED TO
ABRAHAM LINCOLN'S
WIDOW BY 40,000
FRENCH CITIZENS
—*EACH OF WHOM
CONTRIBUTED 2 SOUS*

THE CROSS WAS A SYMBOL REVERED BY THE ZAPOTEC INDIANS OF MEXICO *CENTURIES BEFORE COLUMBUS VISITED THE WESTERN WORLD*

THE GRAVES OF NOTABLES WERE ALWAYS CONSTRUCTED IN THE SHAPE OF A CROSS

Pierre de VILLARS 1517-1592 BECAME ARCHBISHOP of Vienne, France, in 1575 AND WAS SUCCEEDED IN THAT OFFICE BY 4 NEPHEWS -5 MEMBERS OF THE SAME FAMILY HOLDING THE HONOR FOR 118 CONSECUTIVE YEARS

UNEASY LIES THE HEAD THAT WEARS A CROWN THE PILLOW used by the Sultan of the Maghabul Tribe, of Somaliland, *IS CARVED FROM A SINGLE BLOCK OF WOOD*

SCHOOL IS OUT TEACHER HAS GONE HOME

EPITAPH. ON THE TOMBSTONE OF SCHOOL PRINCIPAL S.B. McCRACKEN in Elkhart, Indiana

THE FIRST WAR MEMORIAL BUILT WITH ENEMY ARMOR

The COLOSSUS of RHODES

ONE OF THE SEVEN WONDERS OF THE ANCIENT WORLD - A COPPER STATUE THAT TOWERED 107 FEET ABOVE THE ISLAND OF RHODES—WAS CONSTRUCTED FROM THE WAR MACHINES ABANDONED BY A SYRIAN ARMY THAT HAD TRIED IN VAIN TO BATTER DOWN THE ISLAND'S FORTIFICATIONS FOR AN ENTIRE YEAR
(304 B.C.)

A SMALL WOODEN ARROW

SHOT FROM A SPECIAL BOW IS USED BY NATIVES OF NEW GUINEA

FOR MEDICINAL BLOODLETTING—
THE STONE TIP OF THE ARROW IS DISCHARGED INTO A VEIN IN THE PATIENT'S ARM

MAALULA
a village near Damascus, Syria, COMPRISES MANY CAVE HOMES BUILT INTO THE SIDE OF A LIMESTONE MOUNTAIN
ITS INHABITANTS STILL SPEAK ARAMAIC, THE LANGUAGE OF CHRIST

A **MONUMENT** ON THE SHORES OF Lloyds Lake, in San Francisco, Calif., ONCE SERVED AS THE ENTRANCE COLUMNS AT THE NOB HILL RESIDENCE OF RAILROAD MAGNATE A.N. TOWNE

THE **EGGS** of Arius Falcarius A **BONEFISH,** ARE HATCHED IN THE FATHER'S MOUTH

An **ARANDA ABORIGINE** of Australia FOR CEREMONIAL DRESS COVERS HIS BODY, FACE AND HAIR WITH FEATHERS ·GLUING THEM ON WITH BLOOD DRAWN FROM HIS OWN ARMS

DANCING **DERVISHES** in the days of the Turkish Empire DANCED FOR HOURS IN A TRANCE IN WHICH THEY WERE COMPLETELY UNCONSCIOUS -YET THEY NEVER BRUSHED AGAINST THEIR FELLOW DANCERS

THE **EMIR** of Kano, in Northern Nigeria, ALWAYS CARRIES 2 SPEARS AS WALKING STICKS— THEY HONOR TWIN EMIRS AND THE SPEAR EACH BRANDISHED AS AN EMBLEM OF THEIR JOINT RULE

ELEPHANTS in Cambodia SERVE AS BUSES BETWEEN NEIGHBORING CITIES *OFTEN CARRY AS MANY AS A DOZEN PASSENGERS*

THE **CEILING** OF THE ROYAL HALL OF THE CASTLE OF Tratzberg, Austria, WAS BUILT BY **7** MASTER CARPENTERS ASSISTED BY **7** JOURNEYMEN FROM LUMBER DELIVERED IN **7** WAGONS —AND THE PROJECT TOOK **7** YEARS AND **7** MONTHS TO CREATE

JOANNE WINSHIP (1645-1707) of Cambridge, Mass., WAS AMERICA'S FIRST WOMAN SCHOOL-TEACHER

STRANGE INSCRIPTIONS FOUND ON ROCKS IN THE VALLEY OF FIRE STATE PARK, NEVADA, BELIEVED TO HAVE BEEN PLACED THERE BY ANCIENT PUEBLO INDIANS *HAVE NEVER BEEN DECIPHERED*

YVES GALLOT A FRENCHMAN WHO WALKED A TOTAL OF 620,000 MILES IN COMPETITIONS ONCE OUTWALKED A RELAY OF 2 HORSES -COVERING 296 MILES IN 50 HOURS AND WINNING THE RACE BY A FULL MILE Nice, 1897

"HOLY POLES" ARE ERECTED BY ARAUCARIAN INDIANS OF Chile IN HOLES FILLED WITH SILVER COINS -BUT THEY ARE CONSIDERED SO SACRED THAT NO ONE HAS EVER ATTEMPTED *TO STEAL THE MONEY*

GENERAL ARMAND-LOUIS de GONTAUT-BIRON (1747-1793) of France, SENTENCED TO THE GUILLOTINE BY A FRENCH REVOLUTIONARY TRIBUNAL, REQUESTED A GLASS OF WINE WHICH HE PRESENTED TO THE EXECUTIONER, SAYING: *"YOU NEED COURAGE IN YOUR PROFESSION"*

A FIG TREE near El Palancar, Spain, THAT GREW FROM A STAFF *PLUNGED INTO THE GROUND BY ST. PETER OF ALCANTARA*

ROBERT H. LITTLETON of Salisbury, Md., A ONE-ARMED GOLFER SCORED A HOLE-IN-ONE Elks Golf Course, Salisbury, Md.

THE **WEATHER THISTLE** FORECASTS BAD WEATHER BY FOLDING ITS BLOSSOM

CLEMENS von LAPP
AN OFFICIAL OF BONN, GERMANY,
IN the 18th century
WAS THE FATHER OF 9 DAUGHTERS BUT
ONLY THE ELDEST EVER MARRIED
BECAUSE VON LAPP REFUSED TO LET
ANY OF THEM WED UNTIL ALL THEIR
OLDER SISTERS HAD BEEN MARRIED

THE **CASTLE** OF **RAROGNE** Switzerland
WAS CONVERTED INTO
A CHURCH IN 1512
AFTER HAVING SERVED
AS A CASTLE
FOR 244 YEARS

KNIGHTS in medieval times
OFTEN FLOATED ACROSS LAKES AND STREAMS BY ATTACHING TO THE
FLANKS OF THEIR HORSES *INFLATED GOAT SKINS*

LANCE SKUTHORPE
famed Australian horseman
RODE 7 WILD HORSES IN A PERIOD
OF 7 CONSECUTIVE MINUTES
WITHOUT EVER BEING THROWN

RICHARD WHITNEY
(1776-1815) of
Petersham, Mass,
BECAME
CLERK OF
THE VERMONT
HOUSE OF
REPRESENTATIVES
*AT THE
AGE OF
16*

HEIFER
BORN WITH
2 TAILS
-ONE GROWING
OUT OF ITS
HEAD
Owned by
Larry L. Roberts,
Chalmette, La.

EMPRESS BARBARA

WIDOW OF EMPEROR SIGISMUND I, of Germany SUPPORTED HERSELF DURING THE LAST 7 YEARS OF HER LIFE BY *CLAIMING TO BE AN ALCHEMIST* SHE FUSED COPPER AND ARSENIC AND SOLD THE RESULTANT METAL AS SILVER, AND INCREASED THE WEIGHT OF GOLD INGOTS BY ADDING SILVER AND COPPER (1444-1451)

THE ROCK THAT WAS SPLIT BY A PIT

A BOULDER ON THE CAMPUS OF MICHIGAN STATE COLLEGE THAT WAS SPLIT BY A TREE THAT *GREW FROM A CHERRY PIT*

THE SCHOOL-TEACHER *NATURAL STONE SCULPTURE* Coolah Valley, Australia

ELEPHANT ROCK Nemours, France, *NATURAL STONE FORMATION*

A **CHAPEL** in Krems, Austria, LOCATED IN THE *BAY WINDOW OF A HOUSE*

MEN in ancient Japan AS WELL AS WOMEN LEARNED TO WAVE FANS GRACEFULLY *—BUT ONLY NOBLEMEN WERE PERMITTED TO CARRY FANS CONTAINING 25 LEAVES*

THE **BIRD'S NEST MUSHROOM** LOOKS EXACTLY LIKE A BIRD'S NEST AND CONTAINS HALF A DOZEN SPORES THAT *LOOK LIKE TINY EGGS*

THE **HOUSE OF THE GOLDEN BALL** in Vienna, Austria, STILL DISPLAYS THE CANNONBALL WHICH SMASHED THROUGH ITS ROOF DURING A TURKISH SIEGE *285 YEARS AGO*

THE STONE BEAR near Palau, Sardinia, *NATURAL ROCK FORMATION*

THE FIRST RAILROAD IN AMERICA
WOODEN RAILS WERE LAID BY THOMAS LEIPER IN 1809 BETWEEN A QUARRY AT CROWN CREEK, PA., AND A BOAT LANDING AT RODLEY'S CREEK —A DISTANCE OF 3/4 OF A MILE — OVER WHICH STONE WAS TRANSPORTED IN A HORSE-DRAWN WAGON

LAURENT ÉTIENNE RONDET
(1717-1785) of Paris, France, TAUGHT HIMSELF HEBREW *AT THE AGE OF 7* BY SETTING ALL THE TYPE FOR A HEBREW GRAMMAR, AND THROUGHOUT HIS LIFE HE DEVOTED 15 HOURS A DAY TO STUDYING

The WATERBEAR
CAN ENDURE TEMPERATURES RANGING FROM **207 DEGREES ABOVE ZERO, FAHRENHEIT, TO 317 DEGREES BELOW ZERO**

A TWISTED WILLOW
near Lhasa, Tibet, IS BELIEVED BY TIBETANS TO HAVE BEEN SO SHAPED *BY THE WRITHING EFFORTS OF A GOD TO ESCAPE THAT ABODE* EVERY PASSERBY ADDS ANOTHER STONE TO A PILE OF ROCKS BENEATH THE TREE

PHILIBERT GUENEAU (1720-1785)
FAMED FRENCH NATURALIST
SPENT ONE HOUR EACH MORNING-
EVERY DAY OF HIS ADULT LIFE
*SINGING MADRIGALS AT THE TOP
OF HIS VOICE* - ONE MORNING HE
COMPLETED HIS SONG AND DROPPED
DEAD

THE WATERFALL OF BOUINENC
France
COMPRISES 8 SEPARATE DROPS

EVERY TURKEY HEN
RAISED BY IGNATZ VON ROLL
of Morsbroich, Germany,
WORE AN ELABORATE TURKISH
TURBAN - IN THE BELIEF THAT
SUCCESSIVE GENERATIONS OF
TURKEYS WOULD BE HATCHED
*WITH A TURBAN DESIGN
ON THEIR HEADS*

A **WAR MEDAL**
GIVEN ALL
ENGLISH
SOLDIERS WHO
FOUGHT UNDER
CROMWELL IN
THE BATTLE OF
DUNBAR, SCOTLAND,
DEPICTS THE
ENTIRE ENGLISH
PARLIAMENT

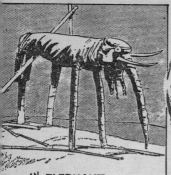

AN ELEPHANT

FASHIONED FROM GRASS AND STICKS MUST BE MAINTAINED OVER THE GRAVE OF ANY MEMBER OF THE LHOTA NAGA TRIBE, OF ASSAM, WHO HAS KILLED AN ELEPHANT —AS LONG AS ANY DESCENDANT OF THE MAN STILL LIVES

THE PASTOR WHO NEVER SPENT A CENT ON HIMSELF

THE REV. URS KREIENBÜHL
PASTOR OF MALTERS, GERMANY, FOR 38 YEARS

WORE ONLY HAND-ME-DOWNS AS CLOTHING AND ATE ONLY THE FOOD GIVEN HIM BY MEMBERS OF THE PARISH—

WHEN HE DIED IN 1803 IT WAS DISCOVERED THAT HIS LIFE'S SAVINGS OF $18,000 HAD BEEN BEQUEATHED TO THE CONGREGATION FOR CONSTRUCTION OF A NEW CHURCH

QUEEN CATHERINE de MEDICI

(1519-1589) of France
WAS THE FIRST EUROPEAN WOMAN TO USE TOBACCO
SHE GROUND IT UP AND USED IT AS SNUFF

HEART in the ancient Egyptian hieroglyphics

IS PORTRAYED IN 2 WAYS —ONE MEANING AN ANIMAL'S HEART AND THE OTHER INDICATING A HUMAN HEART

THE **DRUMS** USED BY THE MAURITANIANS OF the Sahara Desert *ACTUALLY ARE GREAT POTS COVERED WITH LEATHER* THEY MUST BE HEATED BESIDE A BLAZING FIRE BEFORE EACH USE —TO CONTRACT THE DRUMHEAD

A DOG REALLY WAS THIS MAN'S BEST FRIEND! JOHN CRAIG (1512-1600) of Edinburgh, Scotland, PENNILESS AND FRIENDLESS IN VIENNA AND FLEEING A DEATH SENTENCE, WAS AIDED BY A STRAY DOG— *WHICH BROUGHT HIM A WALLET CONTAINING SUFFICIENT MONEY TO PAY FOR HIS TRIP HOME*

HYDRACHNA GEOGRAPHICA A WATER MITE HAS 5 EYES —ONE IN THE CENTER OF ITS BODY

THE **PYRAMID TEMPLE** OF Xochiquetzal, Mexico, WAS CONSTRUCTED OF HUGE GRANITE BLOCKS PUT INTO PLACE WITHOUT MORTAR— YET *NOT A SINGLE BLOCK HAS SHIFTED IN 700 YEARS*

THE OLDEST MOSQUE IN THE WORLD
THE MOSQUE OF DJENNAD in Yemen
THE ONLY STRUCTURE IN THAT
VANISHED CAPITAL OF SOUTHERN YEMEN
STILL STANDING WAS BUILT IN 632
—JUST 10 YEARS AFTER CREATION
OF THE MOSLEM RELIGION

COLUMBUS
BASED HIS
CONCEPTION OF
THE WORLD ON
*AN IMAGINARY
MAN IN THE SKY*

HE ENVISIONED
THE HEAD AND FEET
AS THE HIGHER AND
LOWER MERIDIANS,
THE WAIST AS THE
POLAR REGION AND
DIAGONAL LINES
PASSING THROUGH
THE SHOULDERS
AS THE 4
CARDINAL
DIRECTIONS

MRS. **CHRISTIAN ALMER**,
of Grindelwald, Switzerland,
WHO HAD NEVER BEFORE CLIMBED A MOUNTAIN,
CELEBRATED HER 50TH WEDDING ANNIVERSARY
WITH HER 70-YEAR-OLD HUSBAND—A VETERAN GUIDE—
BY ASCENDING THE 12,166-FOOT WETTERHORN!

THE
**SNOW
PETREL**
a
BIRD OF
Adelie Land, in
the Antarctic,
INCUBATES ITS EGGS IN AN IGLOO
IT BUILDS IN THE SNOW

THE **SANCTUARY** OF **DURGA** near Mammalapuram, India, WAS LABORIOUSLY CARVED FROM A *SINGLE BOULDER*

ALTARS MADE OF FLAGS, SPEARS AND STAVES ARE ERECTED BY TIBETAN TRAVELERS ON PEAKS IN THAT MOUNTAINOUS COUNTRY IN *GRATITUDE FOR SAFE JOURNEYS*

GRÉTRY (1741-1813) celebrated French composer SHORTLY BEFORE HE DIED COMPOSED THE REQUIEM MASS *FOR HIS OWN FUNERAL*

ELIZABETH RANDLES (1800-1829) of Wrexham, Wales, PLAYED THE HARP AT CONCERTS BEFORE ROYALTY *BEFORE SHE WAS 2 YEARS OF AGE*

WILLIAM CUSHING
(1732-1810)
APPOINTED CHIEF JUSTICE OF THE UNITED STATES BY PRESIDENT WASHINGTON IN 1795, *RESIGNED AFTER ONE WEEK ON THE EXCUSE OF POOR HEALTH -YET HE RETURNED IMMEDIATELY TO HIS FORMER POST AS SENIOR ASSOCIATE JUSTICE OF THE COURT AND SERVED IN THAT CAPACITY FOR 15 YEARS*

CLASSROOMS in Luxembourg ARE OFTEN LOCATED IN THE OPEN AIR *IN THE DENSE FORESTS*

THE BY-THE-WIND-SAILOR WHICH HAS A CREST THAT SERVES AS A SAIL, *ACTUALLY COMPRISES HUNDREDS OF INDIVIDUAL ORGANISMS*

THE "ROBERT E. LEE" A BLOCKADE RUNNER PURCHASED BY THE CONFEDERACY IN ENGLAND *ELUDED THE TIGHT UNION BLOCKADE 21 TIMES*

Children in the Kasauli Tribe in the Himalaya region of India ARE LULLED TO SLEEP BY PLACING THEM UNDER A BAMBOO SPOUT WHICH *CONTINUOUSLY POURS WATER ON THE CHILD'S HEAD*

CHARLES-CLAUDE HERMAN (1762-1840) the French biographer RESCUED FROM JUNK DEALERS 18,000 BOOKS SEIZED DURING THE FRENCH REVOLUTION *AND WROTE ALL HIS OWN MANUSCRIPTS ON THE NARROW OUTSIDE SPINES OF THESE VOLUMES*

ZAKHAI BRE MA NE in the language of the Kacharis of India *MEANS "18"* THE KACHARIS HAVE NO NUMERAL HIGHER THAN 7 AND 18 IS WRITTEN: *4X4 PLUS 2*

THE **MONARCH** WHO COULD NOT ESCAPE HIS PROPHECY *KING ALEXANDER I* of Epirus WARNED BY AN ORACLE THAT HE WOULD DIE ON THE ACHERON *LEFT HIS COUNTRY TO AVOID THE LOCAL RIVER OF THAT NAME* FATALLY WOUNDED IN A BATTLE IN ITALY IN 326 B.C. THE KING LEARNED THAT THE RIVER BESIDE WHICH HE LAY ALSO WAS NAMED *THE ACHERON!*

WIDOWS' GARB FISHERMEN'S WIVES in Nazaré, Portugal, CONSIDER THEIR HUSBANDS IN SUCH DANGER AT SEA THAT WHENEVER THE MEN ARE AWAY *THE WOMEN WEAR MOURNING BLACK*

THE **CATERPILLAR** OF THE VICEROY BUTTERFLY EMERGES FROM THE EGG THROUGH A HOLE BORED IN THE SHELL *THEN EATS THE SHELL TO CONCEAL ITS PRESENCE FROM PREDATORS*

AFRICAN WATERBUCK
ARE WARNED OF DANGER
BY FLOCKS OF PLOVERS
*-WHICH FLY OVERHEAD AND
SERVE AS SENTRIES*

PAO CH'ENG

a judge of Anhui, China,
WAS DEIFIED AFTER HIS
DEATH IN 1062 BY THE CHINESE
BECAUSE OF HIS LIFELONG
CONTRIBUTION TO JUDICIAL
DIGNITY *BY NEVER SMILING*

THE **CHAPEL**
of **NOTRE DAME** de la **LIESSE**
in Villeneuve sur-Lot, France,
WHICH CLINGS TO THE SIDE OF A
BRIDGE, *HAS PROJECTED OVER THE
RIVER LOT FOR 700 YEARS*

THE **PEARL FISH**
LIVES INSIDE A SEA CUCUMBER,
INTO WHICH IT ALWAYS BACKS
-TO BE READY FOR A SWIFT EXIT

Ellen AND John JONES of Dymock, England, CELEBRATED THEIR 76th WEDDING ANNIVERSARY

THE BALANCING BLOCK Cape Colonna, Calabria, Italy, A HUGE PIECE OF MASONRY BALANCING ON THE ONLY REMAINING WALL OF THE RUINED PAGAN TEMPLE OF HERA LACINA FOR 1,500 YEARS

MYRA BROOKS WELCH (1878-1959) of La Verne, Calif., SO CRIPPLED BY ARTHRITIS THAT SHE WAS CONFINED TO A WHEEL CHAIR, COMPOSED 3 BOOKS OF POETRY BY LABORING FOR 20 YEARS TOUCHING THE KEYS OF HER TYPEWRITER WITH THE RUBBER TIPS OF 2 PENCILS

THE CREDIT CANE
A CANE-ROD MARKED AT INTERVALS IS STILL USED IN Alpujarra, Spain, TO KEEP TRACK OF THE AMOUNT OF BREAD SOLD ON CREDIT—THE SELLER AND BUYER EACH KEEP A SIMILAR TALLY

STEVE KERRO, A RESIDENT OF INDIANAPOLIS, INDIANA, INJURED IN AN AUTOMOBILE ACCIDENT NEAR BREEZEWOOD, PENNSYLVANIA, WAS TRANSPORTED TO A HOSPITAL IN BERKELEY SPRINGS, W. VIRGINIA, IN AN AMBULANCE FROM MARYLAND
August 4, 1967

THE **NUN** AND **THE MONK** near Vigilia, France, 2 REMARKABLE NATURAL-ROCK FORMATIONS

THE DRUNKARD'S FOUNTAIN
in Rome, Italy
A 16th CENTURY CITIZEN NAMED ABONDIO RIZIO WAS INTOXICATED SO OFTEN *THAT HIS LIKENESS IS CONDEMNED TO SUPPORT A WATER BARREL THROUGH ALL ETERNITY*

HERMANN GOLDSCHMIDT
(1802-1866)
A GERMAN PAINTER RESIDING IN PARIS, FRANCE, BECAME A CELEBRATED ASTRONOMER BY GAZING AT THE SKY THROUGH A SMALL TELESCOPE *FROM THE WINDOW OF A PARISIAN CAFÉ* HE DISCOVERED **14 NEW PLANETS**

WOMEN in India STILL THRESH GRAIN BY FLAILING THE GROUND WITH BUNDLES OF STALKS *-A PROCESS THAT LOSES A GREAT PART OF THE CROP*

THE **WATERFALL** of GANDARA near Santander, Spain, FORMS THE OUTLINE OF A HORSE

THE PALACE OF JUSTICE of Bar-le-Duc, France, WAS BUILT AS A PRIVATE DWELLING IN THE 16th CENTURY, BECAME THE CITY HALL IN 1752, WAS TURNED INTO A MUSEUM IN 1816, AND HAS BEEN A COURTHOUSE FOR THE LAST HALF CENTURY

THE ASTROLOGER WHO COULD NOT ESCAPE HIS OWN PROPHECY OF DOOM FRANCESCO GIUNTINI (1523-1590) WHO AS A YOUTH IN FLORENCE, ITALY, HAD PREDICTED THE DAY AND HOUR OF HIS OWN DEATH BY VIOLENCE, ATTEMPTED TO ESCAPE THAT FATE AT THE PROPHESIED TIME BY LOCKING HIMSELF IN THE LIBRARY OF HIS HOME IN LYON, FRANCE—AT THE VERY HOUR HE HAD PREDICTED, A HEAVY STACK OF BOOKS FELL ON HIS HEAD—KILLING HIM INSTANTLY

THE ORANGETTE A CANDY BOWL manufactured in Spa, Belgium, HAD ORANGE PEEL MIXED INTO THE POTTERY —WHICH GAVE IT AN IMPERISHABLE FRAGRANCE

THE FIRETAIL-FINCH of Australia: NEVER ENTERS HIS NEST UNTIL HE HAS UTTERED A CALL AT THE ENTRANCE AND RECEIVED ASSURANCE FROM HIS MATE INSIDE THAT IT IS SAFE FOR HIM TO JOIN HER

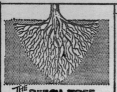

THE **BEECH TREE** HAS ROOTS SHAPED *LIKE A HEART*

A **BATHTUB** INVENTED IN GERMANY IN 1900 GENTLY ROCKED ITS OCCUPANT.

THE **CHURCH** of **TINOS** in Greece TWICE EACH YEAR IS VISITED BY THOUSANDS OF PILGRIMS WHO BELIEVE THAT THEIR AILMENTS WILL BE *CURED BY SLEEPING ON ITS FLOOR*

JOE HODGINI, a celebrated German circus rider, PERFORMED FOR **34** YEARS FOR **$476** A MONTH *— NEVER HAVING RECEIVED EITHER A RAISE OR REDUCTION IN PAY*

THE **BOOKKEEPING LEDGER** of Tangsa natives on the border of Burma and India **IS A BAMBOO CHAIN—** EACH TIME AN INSTALLMENT ON A DEBT IS PAID ONE LINK OF THE CHAIN IS BURNED

THE **MURDERER** WHO DISCOVERED THAT JUSTICE IS **NOT BLIND!**

WILLIAM WILLIAMS of Lick Fort Creek, Alabama, WHO MURDERED HIS FRIEND IN A SIMULATED HUNTING ACCIDENT TWICE ESCAPED FROM PRISON *BUT WAS RECAPTURED WHEN HE WAS STRICKEN BLIND BOTH TIMES — AS SOON AS HE HAD LEFT HIS CELL!* EACH TIME HE RECOVERED HIS SIGHT AFTER BEING RETURNED TO PRISON

SHILLUK TRIBESMEN in Africa SO ADMIRE THEIR CATTLE THAT *THEY PAINT THEIR FACES TO RESEMBLE THEIR BELOVED OXEN*

THE **EGG** of the Mimacraea butterfly of Africa *IS SHAPED LIKE A TURBAN AND STUDDED WITH DEEPLY RECESSED FACETS*

THE CONTRARY WELL OF SIERENTZ, France.
IT YIELDS WATER FREELY DURING PERIODS OF EXTREME DROUGHT — YET WHEN THERE IS AMPLE RAINFALL THIS WELL ALWAYS GOES DRY

THE WOODEN CALENDAR of the Mosangs of India HAS HOLES AND WOODEN PLUGS TO MARK OFF ITS 8-DAY WEEKS, 27-DAY MONTHS AND 12-MONTH YEARS

TUAREG WARRIORS of the Sahara Desert STEER THEIR CAMELS BY TOUCHING THE NECK WITH THEIR BARE FEET — SO BOTH HANDS WILL BE FREE FOR FIGHTING

THE FIRST LIFEBOAT
"THE ORIGINAL" A LIFEBOAT BUILT IN TYNEMOUTH, ENGLAND, 179 YEARS AGO IT WAS 30 FEET LONG AND MADE BUOYANT WITH CORK

THE **MARQUIS d'ANTONELLE** (1747-1817)
noted French author
COULD NOT WRITE UNLESS HE WAS HOLDING
A COLD DISH AGAINST THE BACK OF HIS NECK
*HIS DESK WAS ALWAYS PILED
HIGH WITH CHILLED CROCKERY*

THE **WATER**
of Lake Okataina, N.Zealand,
IS SO PURE IT IS
*USED AS A SUBSTITUTE
FOR DISTILLED WATER
IN BATTERIES*

THE **CHURCH OF ST. GEORGE** in Schenna, Italy,
WAS BUILT IN THE 15th CENTURY BY A POOR FARMHAND NAMED
JOHANN KREBIS—*WHO USED HIS ENTIRE LIFE'S SAVINGS
TO CONSTRUCT IT*

THE THREAD-FINNED FISH of the Amazon IS THE ONLY FISH THAT LAYS ITS EGGS *OUT OF WATER* - IT LEAPS AND DEPOSITS THE EGGS ON FOLIAGE OVERHANGING THE RIVER

FARMHOUSES in Yemen OFTEN COMBINE THE BARN AND HOUSE, WITH THE FAMILY *LIVING ABOVE THE LIVESTOCK*

THE MAN WHO VALUED FRIENDSHIP ABOVE RICHES
Sir GEORGE BOOTH (1622-1684) OFFERED $100,000 FOR HELPING TO RESTORE KING CHARLES II TO HIS THRONE - WAIVED HALF HIS REWARD FOR THE PRIVILEGE OF HAVING **8 FRIENDS RAISED TO THE RANK OF NOBLEMEN**

THE WATER SCORPION WHILE CATCHING FISH UNDERWATER BREATHES *THROUGH A SNORKEL IN ITS TAIL*

A **BULL** THAT WAS BORN WITH 6 LEGS - AND GREW 2 MORE LEGS AT THE AGE OF 6 MONTHS

ULRICH von LICHTENSTEIN
(1200-1275) famed German troubadour
COMPOSED POETRY THAT WAS
WIDELY ACCLAIMED - *YET HE
COULD NEITHER READ NOR WRITE*
HE HAD TO DICTATE HIS
POEMS TO A SECRETARY

from an
old print.

Aconite
BY ORDER OF
EMPEROR TRAJAN
(98-117) COULD NOT
BE GROWN IN
ROME UNDER
PAIN OF DEATH
*BECAUSE WIVES
USED THEM TO
BREW A POISON
TO DO AWAY WITH
THEIR HUSBANDS*

ONLY ROYALTY
in medieval times
COULD DINE AT A TABLE
WITH A DOUBLE CLOTH
*- ONE TABLECLOTH ON
TOP OF ANOTHER -*
A COMMONER CAUGHT
USURPING THIS ROYAL
PREROGATIVE WOULD
FORFEIT HIS RIGHT TO
USE ANY TABLECLOTH FOR
THE REST OF HIS LIFE

THE
SNAIL HAWK
of British Guiana
EATS NOTHING
BUT SNAILS

**KAROLINA
OLLSON**
of Ökna, Sweden,
SLEPT CONTINUOUSLY FOR 32 YEARS
*-AWAKENING IN 1908 ONLY A FEW DAYS
AFTER THE DEATH OF HER MOTHER*

THE **UNION CHURCH** of Marble, Colo., WAS MOVED 30 MILES TO ITS PRESENT SITE FROM ASPEN AND WAS USED FOR SERVICES *BY 3 DIFFERENT DENOMINATIONS*

THE **MILITARY CLOAK** WORN BY KING CHARLES XII of Sweden WHEN HE WAS SLAIN AT FREDERIKSTEN, NORWAY, IS ON VIEW IN THE ROYAL ARMORY IN STOCKHOLM

—STILL SOILED BY THE MUD IN WHICH THE MONARCH FELL 250 YEARS AGO

AN **EARLY TROLLEY TERMINAL** IN HAMBURG, GERMANY, CONSTRUCTED IN 1900 *WAS A CAST-IRON PAGODA—STILL PRESERVED AS A LANDMARK*

PAINTED COPPER PLATES WERE USED BY COAST INDIANS OF BRITISH COLUMBIA *AS MONEY.* IN FESTIVE CELEBRATIONS IT WAS CUSTOMARY TO SHOW DISREGARD FOR MONEY *BY THROWING THE PLATES ONTO BONFIRES*

LIEUTENANT SHAMBURG
of the 2nd U.S. Dragoons
and
ADOLPH CUVILLIER, A CIVILIAN,
STAGED A DUEL ON HORSEBACK
IN NEW ORLEANS IN 1836,
CHARGING AT EACH OTHER
WITH SABERS—*YET BOTH
OPPONENTS EMERGED UNHURT*

A **SUNDIAL**
CONSTRUCTED
BY A. ZEELFT,
in the
Netherlands,
in 1572
*IN THE SHAPE
OF A CROSS*
THE LID SERVED
AS A POINTER,
WITH THE HOURS
INDICATED BY LINES
ON THE SIDES

HARVEY TOMPKINS
of Eureka, Utah,
SHOT AT POINT-BLANK
BY A NEIGHBOR IN A
DISPUTE OVER A
BOUNDARY FENCE, ESCAPED
UNHARMED WHEN THE
BULLET LODGED IN A
*PLUG OF CHEWING TOBACCO
IN HIS SHIRT POCKET* (1884)

COWS of Myednyi Island, off Kamchatka, Russia,
BECAUSE THEY FEED EXCLUSIVELY ON FISH
*PRODUCE MILK WITH SUCH A FISHY
TASTE THAT ONLY NATIVES OF
THE ISLAND CAN DRINK IT*

MEMORIAL TO A MACHINE
THE FIRST STEAM ENGINE in Bielefeld, Germany, A 6 H.P. ENGINE USED BY A DYER AND POWERED BY HORSES FOR LACK OF COAL WAS USED FOR 60 YEARS AND THEN DEDICATED AS A MONUMENT TO ITSELF

THE **GREAT SILVER BEETLE** IS STRICTLY A VEGETARIAN -YET ITS LARVA IS CARNIVOROUS

THE **MONARCH** WHO COULDN'T ESCAPE HIS FATE
EMPEROR ANASTASIUS I of Byzance WARNED THAT HE WOULD BE KILLED BY LIGHTNING, ALWAYS SOUGHT SHELTER DURING ELECTRICAL STORMS- YET A CEILING COLLAPSED AND CRUSHED HIM TO DEATH *WHILE HE COWERED IN AN OLD HOUSE DURING A THUNDERSTORM*
(518)

NATIVES of Ecuador and Peru OFTEN FISH IN DEEP WATER *WHILE SITTING ASTRIDE BUNDLES OF REEDS*

A **FIRE** ENGINE in Bloomingdale, New Jersey, BURST INTO FLAMES ON ITS WAY TO ANSWER AN ALARM IN 1913, BUT ITS DRIVER, FRANK MILLER, EXTINGUISHED THE FIRE, REPAIRED THE DAMAGED CARBURETOR, AND STILL *MANAGED TO REACH THE BURNING BUILDING TO WHICH HE HAD BEEN SUMMONED*

LITIGANTS AMONG THE MOUNTAIN TRIBES of Kenya, Africa, CAN BE REQUIRED TO PROVE THEIR VERACITY BY *RUBBING A RED-HOT SWORD AGAINST THEIR TONGUE*

PETRIFIED ELK ANTLERS DONATED BY CZAR PETER THE GREAT TO THE HORN MUSEUM of Moritzburg Castle, Germany, *WERE MORE THAN 10,000 YEARS OLD*

GLEESON

JEREMIAH GLEESON
DEC. 27, 1793
APR 23, 1904
LYDIA, HIS WIFE
MAR 25, 1817
MAR 7, 1887

TOMBSTONE OF JEREMIAH GLEESON, of Mt. Vernon, Ohio, WHO WAS BORN IN 1793 AND DIED IN 1904 *-HAVING LIVED IN 3 CENTURIES*

JAKOB GRETSER
(1562-1625) the German historian WAS SO MODEST THAT WHEN HIS NATIVE TOWN OF MARKDORF ASKED FOR HIS PORTRAIT TO HANG IN THE CITY HALL, HE SENT A *PICTURE OF A DONKEY*

THE **COPULA** a Chinese junk CONSISTING OF TWO 48-FOOT SHELLS JOINED BY A BRIDGE WAS SAILED BY A CREW OF 5 FROM BORDEAUX, FRANCE, TO NEW YORK-*TRAVERSING A DISTANCE OF 9,000 MILES IN 53 WEEKS* July 23, 1950 to July 30, 1951

THE **BURGLAR ALARM LOCK**

A **LOCK** CONSTRUCTED by Ange Bonin, in 1809, SHAPED LIKE THE FRENCH LEGION OF HONOR AND FILLED WITH COMPRESSED AIR, WHISTLED AND RANG WHEN THE KEY WAS INSERTED, AND WHEN THE KEY WAS WITHDRAWN *EMITTED A LOUD REPORT LIKE A PISTOL SHOT*

THE **REV. J. F. BENSON**
(1843-1933) of Itawamba, Miss., GIVEN A BIBLE BY HIS MOTHER IN 1861 *CARRIED IT WITH HIM EVERY DAY OF HIS LIFE FOR 72 YEARS*

WINDMILL
in Kaltendorf, Germany,
WHICH BURNED TO THE GROUND
IN 1928 WHEN A HIGH WIND
TURNED ITS VANES SO RAPIDLY
*THAT THE WINDMILL
WAS SET AFIRE*

MEN
of the Sango Tribe, of the Congo,
TAKE PRIDE IN THEIR ELABORATE
HAIRDOS AND ARE BITTERLY
HUMILIATED IF THEY ENCOUNTER
*SOMEONE ELSE WEARING
THE SAME CREATION*

**2 SETS
OF ANTLERS**
ADORN A WALL IN THE
CASTLE OF KRANICHSTEIN,
near Darmstadt, Germany,
STILL ENTANGLED AS A RESULT
OF A BATTLE BETWEEN STAGS
THAT CAUSED THE 2 ANIMALS
TO STARVE TO DEATH
212 YEARS AGO

A
**FRENCH
POSTAGE
STAMP**
ISSUED IN 1937 TO HONOR
AUTHOR RENÉ DESCARTES
HAD TO BE WITHDRAWN BECAUSE
*THE TITLE OF HIS BOOK
ON ANALYTIC GEOMETRY
WAS MISQUOTED*

THE GREAT BELL
OF THE SACRED HEART BASILICA IN PARIS, FRANCE, WHEN IT WAS PUT INTO SERVICE ON NOV. 20, 1895, WAS BAPTIZED BY CARDINAL RICHARD—*IT WAS ATTIRED IN A SNOW-WHITE RUFFLED BAPTISMAL ROBE AND ATTENDED BY A GOD-FATHER AND A GODMOTHER*

BENTON H. DICKSON, Jr.
WHO WAS TOWN CLERK OF Weston, Mass., from 1918 to 1943 *GREW A BEARD EACH WINTER TO KEEP HIS FACE WARM AND SHAVED IT OFF EACH SPRING*

M.W.B.
Nov. 21st 1835
She lived unknown and few could know when Mary ceased to be. But she is in her Grave, and, O! The difference to me.

Epitaph in Mount Auburn Cemetery, Cambridge, Mass.

3 STONE CASTLES
near Mannheim, Germany, EACH BUILT ON A NARROW LEDGE OF ROCK BY DIFFERENT GENERATIONS OF THE DAHN FAMILY -*THE FIRST ONE IN 1100* ALL THE ROOMS, CORRIDORS AND STAIRWAYS WERE HEWN FROM THE SOLID ROCK

THE OLDEST KNOWN GLOVES ARE DEPICTED ON A WALL FRESCO IN THE PALACE OF MINOS, CRETE - AND DATE BACK 2,368 YEARS

Emperor **AKBAR** (1542-1602) greatest of the Mongol rulers of India WAS A MOSLEM, BUT IN AN ATTEMPT TO ACHIEVE A BETTER UNDERSTANDING AMONG 3 FAITHS *WORE THE RELIGIOUS MARK OF HINDUISM ON HIS FOREHEAD AND THE SACRED BELT OF THE ZOROASTRIANS*

THE **STALEST WEDDING CAKES IN THE WORLD** BASQUE WEDDING PROCESSIONS at the border of Spain and France ARE PRECEDED BY HALF A DOZEN HUGE WEDDING CAKES - ALL BUT ONE OF WHICH ARE INEDIBLE FAKES *WHICH HAVE SO BEEN CARRIED IN MARRIAGE FESTIVALS FOR GENERATIONS*

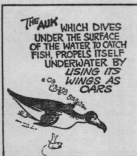

THE **AUK** WHICH DIVES UNDER THE SURFACE OF THE WATER TO CATCH FISH, PROPELS ITSELF UNDERWATER BY *USING ITS WINGS AS OARS*

THE MOST AMAZING MEMORY IN HISTORY

WILLIAM WOODFALL (1746-1803) WROTE VERBATIM REPORTS OF 12-HOUR PARLIAMENTARY DEBATES *YET HE NEVER MADE A SINGLE NOTE* HE WOULD GO HOME AFTER EACH SESSION AND WRITE DOWN THE THOUSANDS OF WORDS FROM MEMORY

THE WEDDING CEREMONY THAT HAS BEEN GOING ON FOR 493 YEARS

THE WEDDING STAGED BY DUKE LUDWIG OF LANDSHUT, GERMANY, FOR HIS SON, GEORG, AND JADWIGA, DAUGHTER OF POLISH KING KAZIMIERZ IV, WAS SO GALA AN AFFAIR THAT IT HAS BEEN PROUDLY RESTAGED IN THE TOWN *EVERY YEAR SINCE 1476*

THE STILT
A LONG-LEGGED BIRD OF NEW ZEALAND HAS A CRY LIKE THE YAPPING OF A DOG

THE HORNBILL
PROTECTS ITS MATE AND THEIR EGGS BY *HIDING THEM IN A HOLLOW TREE AND PLASTERING MUD OVER THE ONLY ENTRANCE*— A TINY SLIT IS LEFT THROUGH WHICH THE HORNBILL PASSES FOOD TO ITS MATE

THE **A-4**

A STEAM LOCOMOTIVE STANDS IN THE CITY PARK IN LAUNCESTON, TASMANIA, AS A MEMORIAL TO THE FACT THAT *IT TRAVELLED 1,000,000 MILES*

ANTONIO **VENIERO**

DOGE OF VENICE FROM 1382 TO 1400 REFUSED TO INTERCEDE FOR HIS OWN SON –SENTENCED TO 2 MONTHS IN JAIL FOR INSULTING A LADY– ALTHOUGH THE BOY BECAME SO ILL THAT *HE DIED IN HIS CELL*

NATIVES of Somaliland PROTECT THEIR HEADS FROM THE HOT SUN **WITH CLAY HAIRDOS** IT ALSO BLEACHES THE HAIR RED AND CLEANS THE SCALP

THE **SHELLS** OF EVERY EGG CONSUMED IN KLEINICH, GERMANY, DURING THE 49-DAY PERIOD BETWEEN EASTER SUNDAY AND WHITSUNDAY ARE CARRIED IN THE LOCAL WHITSUNDAY PROCESSION EACH YEAR - *THREADED INTO 2 GREAT GARLANDS*

THE EGGS ARE LEFT UNBROKEN BY BLOWING THEIR CONTENTS OUT THROUGH 2 HOLES IN EACH SHELL

THE **STAR SNAIL** A SHELL-LESS SNAIL OF THE NORTH SEA *HAS GILLS SHAPED LIKE A STAR*

GEORGES SIMENON WHO HAS BEEN CALLED THE GREATEST LIVING FRENCH NOVELIST HAS WRITTEN UNDER 17 DIFFERENT NOMS DE PLUME *MORE THAN 450 BOOKS* HE ONCE WROTE A COMPLETE NOVEL IN 25 HOURS

CANVASBACK DUCKLINGS ARE OFTEN ABANDONED BY THE MOTHER DUCK BEFORE THEY HAVE LEARNED TO FLY - *ONE OF THE BROOD TAKES OVER AS SUBSTITUTE MOTHER*

THE **MONASTERY OF PALEOKASTRIZZA** on the island of Corfu, in Greece, *ALWAYS BURIES ITS MONKS UPRIGHT*

THE **COLONEL** WHO FOUND YOU CAN'T PROVE YOUR BOSS WRONG
COLONEL QUINTUS ICILLIUS (1709-1786) of Prussia ORIGINALLY WAS NAMED GOTTLIEB GUICHARD, BUT HE WAS FORCED BY KING FREDERICK THE GREAT TO BECOME QUINTUS ICILLIUS AFTER THE COLONEL HAD WON A BET FROM KING FREDERICK *WHO HAD MISTAKENLY INSISTED THERE WAS A MILITARY OFFICER NAMED ICILLIUS*

A **CHINESE REBUS** PAINTED ON OLD PORCELAIN DEPICTS A BAT AND 2 PEACHES – EXPRESSING A WISH FOR "COMPLETE HAPPINESS AND LONGEVITY"

THE **GRAVE** of the Perkins family in Mt. Auburn Cemetery, Cambridge, Mass., IS ETERNALLY GUARDED BY A STATUE *OF THE FAMILY'S WATCHDOG*

WASH AND DRY—
THE DRY BED of the Paillon River, in Nice, France, IS USED BY LOCAL HOUSEWIVES TO DRY THEIR LAUNDRY *ALTHOUGH THE RIVER WATER OFTEN RETURNS SO SUDDENLY ALL THE LAUNDRY IS WASHED AWAY*

THE SIGNAL DRUM
OWNED BY THE KING OF BAMOUN, IN THE CAMEROONS, IS ORNAMENTED WITH CARVED MONKEYS — *IN THE BELIEF IT THUS ACHIEVES ADDED MAJESTY*

MASAI WARRIORS
of Africa
BELIEVE THEY CAN ASSUME THE WISDOM AND BRAVERY OF AN ANCESTOR BY *WEARING HIS HAIR*

THE DEAD MAN'S HAIR IS BRAIDED IN WITH THE DESCENDANT'S OWN — AND HELD IN PLACE BY RED CLAY

DENDRITES
ROCKS ORNAMENTED WITH TREE DESIGNS PAINTED BY MANGANESE OR IRON SOLUTIONS *WERE LONG MISTAKEN FOR FOSSIL PLANTS*

A **HOLLOW BAOBAB TREE**
WHICH SERVES AS A HUMAN
DWELLING NEAR RUMPI, NYASALAND,
HAS BEEN SHAPED BY NATURE. IN
*THE FORM OF BEAUTIFUL
COLUMNS, PANELS AND CORNICES*

WILLIAM GEORGE TIGHT
(1865-1910) PRESIDENT OF THE
University of New Mexico
COMPILED THE SCHOOL'S FIRST
SONG BOOK AND FOUNDED
ITS SCHOOL OF MUSIC
*-YET HE WAS SO UNMUSICAL
THAT HE COULD NOT EVEN
DISTINGUISH ONE NOTE
FROM ANOTHER*

ISRAEL SILVESTRE
(1621-1691)
WHO BECAME ART TEACHER TO
THE HEIR TO THE FRENCH THRONE IN
1675, WAS SUCCEEDED IN THAT POST
BY HIS SON AND 2 GRANDSONS
*-HIS FAMILY SERVING AS ART
TUTORS TO FUTURE MONARCHS
FOR 134 CONSECUTIVE YEARS*

SHEEPSKIN MONEY
ISSUED BY GOVERNOR ROSS
OF THE KEELING-COCOS
ISLANDS IN THE PACIFIC,
IN 1910, HAD A DIFFERENT
SHAPE FOR EACH OF
THE 6 DENOMINATIONS,
*SO ILLITERATE NATIVES
COULD RECOGNIZE
ITS VALUE*

LAMAS
of Nepal
WHEN THEY BECOME BALD
WEAR AS A BLACK TOUPEE
THE TAIL OF A YAK

SEPTIMIUS SEVERUS
(146-211)
AS A REWARD FOR HIS
ELECTION AS ROMAN
EMPEROR, GAVE EACH OF
HIS 12,000 SOLDIERS
50,000 SESTERCES
— A TOTAL OF
$25,764,000

THE **PILLAR** WHICH SERVED AS A GALLOWS in Grosskrut, Austria, FOR CENTURIES IS STILL PRESERVED AS A MEMORIAL TO THE HUNDREDS OF SINNERS EXECUTED ON IT

LOUIS, DUKE de LONGUEVILLE French military commander CAPTURED BY KING HENRY VIII OF England, IN THE BATTLE OF THE SPURS AND UNABLE TO RAISE HIS RANSOM WAS PERMITTED TO WIN THE MONEY FROM THE MONARCH BY WAGERS AT "CROQUET" (JUNE, 1513)

OPTICAL ILLUSION
CAN YOU FIND THE NAME OF A TOWN IN PARAGUAY IN THIS DESIGN? Ans. *ITA*, A TOWN LOCATED 26 MILES FROM PARAGUAY'S CAPITAL

THE FLYING DRUMMERS
Pigeons WITH AS MANY FEATHERS ON THEIR FEET AS THEY HAVE ON THEIR WINGS AND WITH A CALL THAT SOUNDS LIKE A ROLL OF DRUMS. THEIR FEATHERED HELMET IS SO THICK THEY CAN ONLY LOOK DOWN

A **WEDDING**
AMONG THE KIRGISIANS
of Kazakhstan, Russia,
MUST BE PERFORMED 7 TIMES
*WITH THE ENTIRE FEAST
AND MARRIAGE CEREMONY
REPEATED EACH TIME*

THe **PILLARS**
of the Well Hall, in Heidelberg,
Germany, WERE FORMERLY PART OF
CHARLEMAGNE'S PALACE IN INGELHEIM
- *AND BEFORE THAT HAD DECORATED
THE PALACE OF AN ANCIENT ROMAN
GOVERNOR IN GERMANY IN
THE 1st CENTURY*

UYACOQ
(1860-1924)
AN ALASKAN ESKIMO
DETERMINED TO BECOME
THE FIRST ESKIMO AUTHOR
*FIRST HAD TO CREATE
AN ESKIMO ALPHABET*
ACTUALLY, HE CREATED 2
ALPHABETS, ONE OF SYLLABLES
AND THE OTHER OF PICTURES

BARTOLOMEO PORTUGUES a buccaneer on the Spanish Main WAS UNABLE TO SWIM —YET HE ESCAPED FROM A SHIP IN MID-OCEAN BY CLINGING TO 2 EARTHEN WINE JUGS

THE **MAN** WHO GAVE THE WORLD THE CALENDAR

CNEIUS FLAVIUS a Roman IN 304 B.C. BECAME THE FIRST MAN TO PUBLISH A CALENDAR

BEFORE THAT TIME CALENDARS WERE THE SECRET POSSESSIONS OF PUBLIC OFFICIALS – WHO MANIPULATED THEIR CONTENTS AT WILL

THE BAROMETER WELL of ALTKIRCH, France A WELL, 65 FEET DEEP THAT WARNS OF APPROACHING STORMS *BY BLOWING OUT GUSTS OF AIR*

THE **SACRED HEART BASILICA** in Singapore WAS BUILT AS A FAITHFUL REPLICA OF *THE FAMED BASILICA OF THE SAME NAME IN PARIS, FRANCE*

A **BEAN** (Abrus Precatorius) IS SO UNIFORM IN SIZE IT IS USED IN INDIA *AS A STANDARD OF WEIGHT*

A **STATUE** in Berne, Switzerland, HONORS URS LERBER, WHO RACED 300 MILES FROM BERNE TO PARIS, FRANCE, TO DELIVER A MESSAGE TO KING CHARLES IX of France

THE STATUE HONORS THE RUNNER'S COURAGE, NOT HIS FEAT

WHEN KING CHARLES EXPRESSED ASTONISHMENT THAT THE MESSENGER SENT TO HIM COULD NOT SPEAK FRENCH, URS REPLIED HE WAS *SURPRISED THE MONARCH COULD NOT SPEAK GERMAN*

THE **TOMBSTONE** of Pierre Gaspard, A MOUNTAIN GUIDE IN Saint-Christophe, France, IS A REPLICA OF MT. MEIJE (13,080' HIGH) *WHICH GASPARD WAS THE FIRST MAN TO CLIMB*

PAUL DOUMER (1857 - 1932) AS HIS 13th GOVERNMENT OFFICE, BECAME THE 13th PRESIDENT OF THE 3rd REPUBLIC ON MAY 13, 1931- AT HIS INAUGURATION HE PREDICTED THAT HIS STRING OF 13'S MADE HIM A LIKELY TARGET FOR ASSASSINATION - AND THE FOLLOWING MAY HE WAS ASSASSINATED (FRANCE)

AN AIR FRESHENER COMPRISING A TABLE FOUNTAIN SPRAYING WATER THROUGH A BOUQUET OF FRESH FLOWERS *WAS INVENTED IN 1900 AND SOLD FOR $38*

LUIS de VARGAS (1502-1568) A CELEBRATED PAINTER OF SEVILLE, SPAIN, WAS SO DEVOUT THAT HE WORE A HAIR SHIRT *-AND SPENT 4 HOURS EACH DAY ON A BIER MEDITATING ON DEATH FOR THE LAST 46 YEARS OF HIS LIFE*

THE **CHINESE TUMBLER GOLDFISH** CANNOT SWIM NORMALLY - ITS ONLY MEANS OF MOVEMENT BEING A SERIES OF BACKWARD SOMERSAULTS

THE **DREAM** THAT MIRRORED TRAGIC REALITY

WILLIAM BARNES, A MATE ON THE SAILING SHIP "PETUNIA," HAD A DREAM AT SEA IN WHICH HE SAW HIS AUNT, ELIZA ALLEN, LYING DEAD IN HER HOME IN ST. JOHNS, NEWFOUNDLAND, *1,500 MILES AWAY*- THE HOUR AND DATE OF THE DREAM WAS ENTERED IN THE SHIP'S LOG - AND WHEN BARNES RETURNED HOME HE FOUND HIS AUNT ACTUALLY HAD DIED AT THAT VERY HOUR

CORBIN'S HOTEL in Westerville, Ohio, WAS DEMOLISHED BY **56 POUNDS** OF GUNPOWDER - YET 13 GUESTS ASLEEP IN ITS ROOMS *ESCAPED WITHOUT A SCRATCH* Sept. 15, 1879

MARY CALLINACK

A FISHWIFE of Penzance, England, WALKED **300 MILES** TO VIEW THE HYDE PARK EXPOSITION IN LONDON *AT THE AGE OF 84* 1851

EBON ATOLL IN THE MARSHALL ISLANDS OF THE PACIFIC *IS SHAPED LIKE A HUGE BIRD*

THE WHIRLIGIG WHICH ALWAYS SWIMS AT THE SURFACE CAN *SIMULTANEOUSLY SEE ABOVE AND BELOW THE WATER BECAUSE EACH OF ITS EYES IS DIVIDED INTO 2 SECTIONS*

THE ENGLISH LADIES IS THE NAME OF A GROUP OF ALPINE PEAKS IN THE MONT BLANC REGION BECAUSE THEIR OUTLINE SUGGESTS *A GROUP OF ENGLISH LADIES IN 19th-CENTURY DRESS*

SCHOOLROOMS IN MANY VILLAGES IN NORTHERN CHILE HAVE NO TEACHERS, *SO THE LOCAL POLICEMEN INSTRUCT THE YOUNGSTERS*

LIBERIA
WITH A POPULATION OF ONLY 2,500,000 *LEADS THE WORLD IN SHIPPING TONNAGE* ITS MERCHANT FLEET TOTALS 25,073,338 TONS — MORE THAN THE UNITED STATES, GREAT BRITAIN AND NORWAY

THE TOWN WITHOUT A SINGLE STREET
Sewell
A COMMUNITY ON El Teniente Mountain, Chile, HAS A POPULATION OF 6,000 — BUT IT **HAS NO STREETS OR VEHICLES** *ITS SIDEWALKS CONSIST ENTIRELY OF STAIRWAYS*

CALIPH HESHAM II
(974-1036) of Cordoba
TOOK 3 YEARS TO DECIDE TO ACCEPT THE THRONE OF MOORISH SPAIN — ONLY *TO BE DEPOSED A YEAR LATER*

THE COAT OF ARMS of Tarazona, Spain, CLAIMS THE TOWN WAS FOUNDED BY TUBAL CAIN, A GRANDSON OF METHUSELAH — *WHICH WOULD MAKE THE TOWN 5,972 YEARS OLD*

A RAIN QUEEN

RULES SWAZILAND JOINTLY WITH THE COUNTRY'S KING

BUT SHE IS DEPOSED IF SHE FAILS TO BREW UP A STORM AT THE ANNUAL FEAST OF THE FIRST FRUITS

THE CHURCH OF RÄTTVIK Sweden IS SURROUNDED BY WOODEN CABINS IN WHICH WORSHIPERS WHO LIVED FAR FROM THE EDIFICE *SPENT THE NIGHT BEFORE JOURNEYING HOME*

THE BALANCED ROCK In the Garden of the Gods, Colorado, A HUGE BOULDER *SUPPORTED BY A TINY BASE*

THE **HOUSE OF THE CHAIN** in Pinto, Spain, FOR CENTURIES A SANCTUARY FOR ANY CRIMINAL SAVED FROM IMPRISONMENT AND THE HANGMAN MORE THAN 1,800 MEN

BRIDES in the Wai Wai Tribe on the border of British Guiana and Brazil ACQUIRE HUMILITY BY WEARING A BELT SHAPED LIKE THE HIDE OF A JAGUAR *IN WHICH SCORES OF ANTS HAVE BEEN IMPRISONED*

A **SON-IN-LAW** in the Shona Tribe of S. Africa CAN APPROACH HIS WIFE'S FATHER ONLY WITH HIS KNEES BENT AND HIS HEAD TURNED AWAY

SAUDI ARABIA HAS MODERN TV PROGRAMS —YET MOVIES ARE FORBIDDEN BY LAW

THE **RED BILLED TOUCAN** of British Guiana WHEN SLEEPING COVERS ITSELF WITH ITS LONG BILL AND TAIL

ANN BORODELL,
(1615-1712) of Cork, Ireland,
AT HER MARRIAGE TO GEORGE
DENISON, OF STONINGTON, CONN.,
RECEIVED FROM HER FATHER AS
A DOWRY HER WEIGHT IN
GOLD *- EXACTLY 90 POUNDS*

BRAUNFELS CASTLE
in *Germany*
HAS BEEN OCCUPIED BY
THE SAME FAMILY
-THE PRINCES OF SOLMS-
FOR 722 YEARS

FISHERMEN in India
OFTEN MAKE THEIR RAFTS BY
MERELY LASHING 2 TREE TRUNKS TOGETHER

A WATERFALL
near Millheim, Pa.,
FORMED BY AN INVISIBLE RIVER—
THE RIVER EMERGES AT THAT POINT
FROM BENEATH THE ROCKY CLIFF

from an
old print

THE STRANGEST DINNER PARTY IN HISTORY
GRIMOD de la REYNIÈRE - famed French
gourmet—INVITED 22 FRIENDS TO A
DINNER OF 9 COURSES - EACH COURSE
COMPRISING A DIFFERENT TYPE OF MEAT
AND EACH MEAT BEING PREPARED
IN 22 DIFFERENT WAYS

**ONE OF THE TOUGHEST,
ROUGHEST MARSHALS**
IN AMERICAN HISTORY
WAS A WOMAN—
MISS PHOEBE COUZINS,
of St. Louis, Mo., (1854-1913)
WHO SUCCEEDED HER
FATHER AS U.S. MARSHAL
*WAS FEARED BY
EVERY LAWBREAKER*

CAMEL HEAD ROCK
NATURAL STONE FORMATION
Moshannon Drive, Scotia, Pa.

THE **BELFRY** of the CHURCH OF San Miguel in Tarazona, Spain, TEMPORARILY TOPPED WITH A PYRAMID OF GRAVEL WHEN WAR HALTED CONSTRUCTION IN 1507, HAS STILL NOT BEEN COMPLETED *461 YEARS LATER*

THE **SENTIMENTAL SLAYER** ALI PASHA (1741-1822) the Turkish tyrant of Janina, Greece, BOASTED THAT IN HIS 40 YEARS AS A RULER *HE MURDERED 30,000 MEN, WOMEN AND CHILDREN* -YET HE ALWAYS WEPT AND ASKED FORGIVENESS WHEN HE PICKED A FLOWER

THE **2-TOED SLOTH** HAS 6 VERTEBRAE IN ITS NECK, 1 LESS THAN MOST OTHER MAMMALS -YET THE *3-TOED SLOTH HAS 2 MORE VERTEBRAE THAN OTHER ANIMALS*

THE **GREAT GOLDEN ALTAR** in the Monastery of Miraflores, Spain, ERECTED BY QUEEN ISABELLA OVER THE TOMB OF HER PARENTS, WAS COVERED *WITH THE FIRST GOLD BROUGHT FROM THE NEW WORLD BY COLUMBUS*

TWO SPRINGS ARE LOCATED SIDE BY SIDE in Livadia, Greece —ONE NAMED *THE SPRING OF MEMORY* AND THE OTHER *THE SPRING OF FORGETFULNESS*

HENRY CLAY FRENCH of Heppner, Oreg., IN A PERIOD OF 36 YEARS WORKED FOR 14 DIFFERENT RAILROADS AS ERRAND BOY, TELEGRAPHER, SWITCHMAN, BRAKEMAN, BAGGAGEMAN, CONDUCTOR, FIREMAN, STATION AGENT AND ENGINEER

JERRY HARKNESS of the Indiana Pacers, of Indianapolis, Ind., WON A BASKETBALL GAME BY ONE POINT WITH A 92-FOOT SHOT —JUST BEFORE THE GAME ENDED (Nov. 13, 1967)

THE **JACKKNIFE JUDGE**

JUSTICE OF THE PEACE CHARLES REAUME (1752-1822) of the Green Bay District of Wisconsin WAS SO WELL KNOWN THAT A CONSTABLE HE SENT OUT TO MAKE AN ARREST NEVER CARRIED A BADGE OR WRIT —BUT WAS MEEKLY OBEYED WHEN HE DISPLAYED *THE JUDGE'S JACKKNIFE*

THE CHURCH of ST. GEORGE of Sofia, Bulgaria, WAS BUILT 1,860 YEARS AGO AS A ROMAN BATH FOR EMPEROR TRAJAN

THE BLACK TURBAN SNAIL HAS A SHELL THAT LOOKS LIKE THE MOSLEM HEADGEAR

HORACE GRAY WHO WAS APPOINTED TO THE U.S. SUPREME COURT IN 1881 WAS THE FIRST JURIST OF THAT COURT TO HIRE A LEGAL SECRETARY

CATHEDRAL ROCK NATURAL STONE FORMATION near the U.S. Air Force Academy, Colorado

THE **COYPU**
of South America
HIDES ITS VALUABLE
SHORT-HAIRED FUR
*BENEATH AN OUTER
COAT OF ROUGH HAIR*

THE EARL OF DONEGAL
HAS BEEN KNOWN AS LORD DONEGALL
FOR 290 YEARS BECAUSE IN A COURT
ACTION IN WHICH THE SECOND EARL OF
DONEGAL CLAIMED THE ISLAND OF INCH,
IRELAND, HIS OPPONENT PROTESTED
THAT IF LORD DONEGAL WAS **"GRANTED AN
INCH HE WOULD TAKE AN ELL"** (an old
English measure of 45 inches)

*THE EARL ADOPTED THE SUGGESTION AND
THE FAMILY NAME HAS BEEN DONEGALL
EVER SINCE*

AN **IRON TRIDENT**
EMBLEM OF THE
HINDU GOD SHIVA
STILL STANDS ON THE SITE OF AN
ANCIENT TEMPLE NEAR KATMANDU, NEPAL
*-THE REMAINDER OF WHICH
CRUMBLED TO DUST CENTURIES AGO*

THE
SLOTH
WITH THE
LOWEST BODY
TEMPERATURE OF
ANY MAMMAL (95½°)
*SLEEPS 18 OUT OF
EVERY 24 HOURS*

COW 26 YEARS OLD
owned by Mrs. Sallie Ross, Conroe, Texas

THE MOCKING PIGEON
THE LAUGHER a pigeon found only in Thailand CHUCKLES LIKE A MAN, BARKS LIKE A DOG, AND CAWS LIKE A CROW

A BROWN BEAR
PURSUED IN THE SOUTHERN TYROL IN 1881 CLIMBED 12,802 FEET TO THE PEAK OF MT. ORTLER BY A ROUTE NO MOUNTAINEER HAD BEEN ABLE TO CONQUER

MARGARET THOMPSON
of London, England, WHO DIED IN 1777 WAS SO FOND OF SNUFF THAT AT HER DIRECTION HER COFFIN WAS FILLED WITH THE BEST SCOTTISH SNUFF

CROSSES MADE OF MOUNTAIN ASH ARE FASTENED TO CATTLE ON MAY 1 ON THE ISLE OF MAN TO PROTECT THEM AGAINST WITCHES

THE MOST SENSITIVE ARTIST IN ALL HISTORY

XAVIER SIGALON (1787-1837) a noted French painter, WAS SO HURT BY CRITICISM OF ONE OF HIS PAINTINGS IN 1827 THAT HIS *JET-BLACK BEARD TURNED SNOW-WHITE OVERNIGHT*

JOHN SAYRE of Salem County, N.J., WHO COULD NOT SWIM, WAS RESCUED BY A STRANGER AFTER FALLING FROM A WHARF IN PHILADELPHIA, PA., BUT WHEN HE LEARNED HE OWED HIS LIFE TO THE SON OF A BRITISH COLONEL WHOSE TROOPS HAD MASSACRED SAYRE'S FATHER AND OTHER AMERICANS IN 1778, *HE LEAPED BACK INTO THE WATER* - HE WAS RESCUED THE 2ND TIME WITH GREAT DIFFICULTY

THE ARCH OF MARIA THERESA in Innsbruck, Austria,

ERECTED IN 1765 TO CELEBRATE THE WEDDING OF AUSTRIAN ARCHDUKE LEOPOLD AND PRINCESS MARIA LUDOVICA OF SPAIN IS A MEMORIAL TO BOTH JOY AND SORROW — *THE GROOM'S FATHER, EMPEROR FRANCIS I, WHO DIED DURING THE WEDDING, IS COMMEMORATED ON THE OTHER SIDE OF THE ARCH*

A CLUB PASSED FROM HOME TO HOME IN ANCIENT GERMANY *WAS THE OFFICIAL INVITATION TO ATTEND A COMMUNITY MEETING*

FAILURE TO PASS ON THE CLUB WAS A CRIME

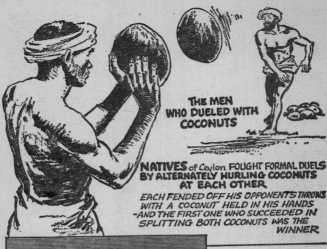

THE MEN WHO DUELED WITH COCONUTS

NATIVES of *Ceylon* FOUGHT FORMAL DUELS BY ALTERNATELY HURLING COCONUTS AT EACH OTHER

EACH FENDED OFF HIS OPPONENT'S THROWS WITH A COCONUT HELD IN HIS HANDS — AND THE FIRST ONE WHO SUCCEEDED IN SPLITTING BOTH COCONUTS WAS THE WINNER

THE **HIPPOPOTAMUS** *WHILE IN THE WATER* OFTEN IS CLEANED OF ALGAE AND DEAD SKIN BY A NUMBER OF CARP-LIKE FISH THAT CLING TO THE HIPPO'S SKIN BY MEANS OF SUCKERS

THE **ENTIRE VILLAGE** OF EPESSES in Switzerland DURING A VIOLENT EARTHQUAKE IN 563 SLID 100 FEET DOWN THE MOUNTAINSIDE — *WITHOUT CRACKING A SINGLE WALL*

THE **SEEDCASE** of the NOON FLOWER (tragopogon pratensis) IS SHAPED LIKE A PARASOL — *WHICH OPENS IN THE SUNSHINE AND CLOSES IN THE RAIN* — THIS ALTERNATE OPENING AND CLOSING MOVES THE SEEDCASE ALONG THE GROUND UNTIL IT FINDS A SUITABLE PLACE TO TAKE ROOT

THE GREAT TOWER of Gavone Castle, in No.11, Italy, IS CONSTRUCTED WITH DIAMOND-SHAPED STONES BECAUSE THE BUILDER'S WIFE FINANCED ITS CONSTRUCTION IN THE 16th CENTURY *BY SELLING HER DIAMOND JEWELRY.*

THE **JURIST** WHO OWED HIS LIFE TO A SINGLE COIN

ASSOCIATE JUSTICE HENRY BALDWIN (1780-1844) OF THE U.S. SUPREME COURT DURING A YOUTHFUL DUEL IN PITTSBURGH, PA., IN 1805 WAS STRUCK OVER THE HEART BY HIS OPPONENT'S SHOT *—BUT WAS SAVED FROM CERTAIN DEATH BECAUSE HE WAS CARRYING A SILVER DOLLAR IN A PURSE IN HIS BREAST POCKET*

WIVES in some Congo tribes WEAR THEIR LIFE SAVINGS IN THE FORM OF A COPPER COLLAR *WHICH WEIGHS AS MUCH AS 44 POUNDS*

THE **VEGETABLE OYSTER** *SALSIFY* LOOKS LIKE A PARSNIP *BUT TASTES LIKE AN OYSTER*

THE **BIGGEST SAND DUNE IN EUROPE** located near Arcachon, France, *IS 350 FEET HIGH*

IT MOVES INLAND AT THE RATE OF 40 FEET A YEAR, ENGULFING THOUSANDS OF TREES ANNUALLY

Spikes of the Scorpion acacia plant of India *ARE USED AS FISHHOOKS AND PINS*

BANANA BEER IS MADE BY THE BUNYORO TRIBESMEN of Uganda, Africa, *WITH THEIR FEET*

COOKED BANANAS, GRASS, WATER AND BANANA STEMS ARE TROD ON FOR HOURS, THEN ALLOWED TO FERMENT—*AND THE WHOLE BREW MUST BE DRUNK WITHIN 24 HOURS*

4 STONE STAGS ADORN THE CORNERS OF Moritzburg Castle, in Germany —BUT THE HEAD OF EACH STAG *HAS A SET OF GENUINE ANTLERS*

THE **TUNNEL OF TREES** PLANE TREES, LINING THE ROAD in Cava dei Tirreni, Italy, HAVE BECOME SO ENTANGLED IN THEIR UPPER BRANCHES *THAT THEY FORM A COVERED PASSAGEWAY*

A *TALISMAN* SHAPED LIKE A SCORPION WORN BY TIBETANS TO PROTECT THEM *FROM NIGHTMARES*

THE MAN WHO WAS KILLED FOR HIS OWN GOOD!

KHEOMURJIAN GOMIDAS the Armenian author WAS FOUND INNOCENT OF A CHARGE OF HIGH TREASON ON OCT. 25, 1707 BY A TURKISH COURT, BUT TO SAVE HIM FROM ASSASSINATION BY POLITICAL FOES *HE WAS SENTENCED TO BE DECAPITATED!*

THE SNOW MARCHERS OF SPAIN

A *PARADE* IS HELD IN TORREJONCILLO EVERY FEB. 24th WITH EVERY PARTICIPANT WEARING A WHITE ROBE TO COMMEMORATE THE BATTLE OF PAVIA IN 1525 IN WHICH SPANISH SOLDIERS FOUGHT IN DEEP SNOW -WEARING WHITE SHEETS AS CAMOUFLAGE

OYSTER SHELLS ARE USED IN THE CAROLINE ISLANDS, IN THE PACIFIC, *AS MONEY*

THE **BELFRY** of the Church of St. Cassiano, in Quinto, Italy, FORMERLY SERVED AS THE TOWER OF A MEDIEVAL CASTLE —ALL BUT THE TOWER OF WHICH WAS DEMOLISHED 100 YEARS BEFORE THE CHURCH WAS BUILT

THE FIELD OF HONOR

FIELD MARSHAL de GUEBRIANT DEFENDING THE BESIEGED TOWN of Guise, France, ALTHOUGH FAR OUTNUMBERED BY A FORCE OF SPANIARDS, OFFERED TO DEMOLISH HIS FORTIFICATIONS AND FIGHT IN THE OPEN IF *THE SPANIARDS WOULD WITHDRAW IF DEFEATED* THE SMALLER FORCE OF FRENCHMEN WERE VICTORIOUS ON THE OPEN FIELD —AND THE SPANIARDS KEPT THEIR WORD AND ABANDONED THE SIEGE

LYNN HOLLINGSWORTH a Canadian hunter, REACHED INTO A WOLF'S DEN ON DAWSON'S ISLAND, *YANKED A WOLF OUT BY THE TAIL AND TOSSED IT A DISTANCE OF 10 FEET* (1935)

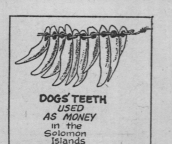

DOGS' TEETH USED AS MONEY in the Solomon Islands

ALEXANDER von MÖRK (1889-1914) IS BURIED IN THE LARGEST ICE CAVE IN THE WORLD, THE GREAT ICE CAVE IN THE Dachstein Mountains, near Salzburg, Austria, WHICH HE DISCOVERED IN 1912 — *2 YEARS BEFORE HE WAS FATALLY WOUNDED IN WORLD WAR I*

FISHERMEN

on the Niger River, in Nigeria, Africa, *FLOAT ON THEIR STOMACHS ON DRIED PUMPKIN SHELLS*

CUPID'S GATE A SQUARE OPENING IN THE ROCK WALL OF VERDEZUN, France, IS BELIEVED TO HAVE THE POWER TO ASSURE ANYONE PASSING THROUGH IT *A HAPPY MARRIAGE WITHIN THE YEAR*

THE NOBLEST RIVER
THE MENAM RIVER in Thailand IS CALLED CHAO PHAYA IN THE SIAMESE LANGUAGE – WHICH MEANS IT HAS BEEN GIVEN THE TITLE OF DUKE AS A REWARD FOR ITS USEFULNESS

GONDOVALD (550-585)
GIVEN THE THRONE OF AQUITANIA, now a part of Southern France, TOOK THE OATH OF OFFICE IN 580 *12 TIMES IN A SINGLE DAY* HE SWORE TO BE A GOOD RULER IN 12 DIFFERENT CHURCHES –BUT HE WAS EXECUTED 5 YEARS LATER

CHILDREN'S FUNERALS in Colombia, in the 19th century, WERE PRECEDED BY GAY GUITAR MUSIC AND THE BODY WAS CARRIED IN A SEATED POSITION ATOP A HIGH POLE, *ATTIRED TO RESEMBLE AN ANGEL*

THE MAN WHO COULD NOT ESCAPE HIS FATE
MARCUS HERENNIUS an officer in ancient Rome NEVER WENT OUTDOORS DURING STORMS BECAUSE A SOOTHSAYER HAD WARNED HIM HE WAS DESTINED TO DIE BY LIGHTNING *HE WAS KILLED BY A LIGHTNING BOLT ON A BRIGHT, SUNNY DAY*

THE GREAT NEBULA OF ANDROMEDA IS SO FAR AWAY THAT ITS LIGHT, TRAVELING 186,000 MILES PER SECOND, DOES NOT REACH THE EARTH *FOR 1,000,000 YEARS*

STYLEPHORUS A DEEP-SEA FISH WITH A TAIL FIN TWICE AS LONG AS ITS BODY, ALWAYS SWIMS VERTICALLY

KING MONGKUT (1804-1868) of Siam WHO WAS THE FATHER OF 82 CHILDREN *WAS THE FIRST SIAMESE IN HISTORY WHO COULD READ AND WRITE ENGLISH*

THE **NEW** COVERED BRIDGE OVER THE AAR RIVER, near Berne, Switzerland, ACTUALLY HAS BEEN STANDING FOR *499 YEARS*

"PRINCE VALIANT" HAS BEEN TOPS WITH THE LADIES FOR 578 YEARS

DUKE JOHN IV (1338-1399) of Brittany *THE ORIGINAL "PRINCE VALIANT"* WAS THE ONLY RULER IN ALL HISTORY TO GRANT WOMEN THE HONOR OF KNIGHTHOOD!

THE BOWING PAGODA near Kiang Hsen, Burma, THE STRUCTURE, 75 FEET HIGH, WAS CONSTRUCTED ON A SLANT *TO INDICATE AN ATTITUDE OF PRAYER*

A **LOCOMOTIVE** PLUNGED INTO A HOLE 200 FEET DEEP THAT SUDDENLY OPENED UP IN THE RAILROAD YARD AT LINDAL, ENGLAND, AND STILL REMAINS THERE COVERED BY DIRT —76 YEARS LATER

ROBERT MICKLE of Baltimore, Md., WAS EMPLOYED BY THE NATIONAL UNION BANK OF MARYLAND *CONTINUOUSLY FOR 73 YEARS*

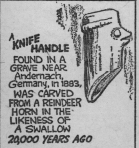

INDIAN WAR ELEPHANTS in the 18th century WENT INTO BATTLE *COMPLETELY ENCASED IN ARMOR*

A **KNIFE HANDLE** FOUND IN A GRAVE NEAR Andernach, Germany, in 1883, WAS CARVED FROM A REINDEER HORN IN THE LIKENESS OF A SWALLOW *20,000 YEARS AGO*

THE IMPRINT OF A HUMAN HAND IN THE CAVE OF GARGAS, IN THE HAUTES PYRÉNÉES, France —MADE 30,000 YEARS AGO

BURNING OF COAL BECAUSE OF THE DANGER OF AIR POLLUTION WAS FORBIDDEN IN 13th-CENTURY ENGLAND

MORGAN BULKELEY (1837-1922) SERVED AS GOVERNOR OF CONNECTICUT FOR 2 YEARS WITHOUT HAVING BEEN A CANDIDATE AND WITHOUT BEING ELECTED THE STATE LEGISLATURE COULD NOT AGREE ON THE VICTOR OF THE GUBERNATORIAL ELECTION IN 1890, SO BULKELEY, AS THE INCUMBENT, CONTINUED IN OFFICE UNTIL 1893

VILLAGES
In Northern Syria CONSISTING OF HUTS MADE ENTIRELY OF CLAY IN THE SHAPE OF GIANT BEEHIVES *HAVE NOT CHANGED IN THOUSANDS OF YEARS.*

THE **TEETH** OF THE TIGER SHARK LIE FLAT AGAINST ITS GUMS WHEN ITS MOUTH IS CLOSED BUT WHEN THE SHARK OPENS ITS JAWS *THE TEETH SPRING ERECT*

NATIVES of the Nicobar Islands, in the Bay of Bengal, India, CELEBRATE THEIR BIRTHDAYS BY DIGGING UP THE SKULLS OF DECEASED KIN AND STAGING A PARADE —TO IMPRESS FRIENDS WITH THEIR ANCESTRY

THE **SHARP-SHINNED HAWK** CAN SWALLOW ITS PREY WHOLE, BUT WHEN IT IS FEEDING A BIRD TO ITS YOUNG *THE HAWK CAREFULLY PLUCKS OUT EVERY FEATHER TO MAKE THE BIRD DIGESTIBLE*

THE **ORACLE** of the Azande Tribe, of the Sudan, ANSWERS QUESTIONS ON MATTERS OF STATE *WITH A PRIMITIVE OUIJA BOARD*

MARSHAL MACMAHON
(1808-1893) who became
President of France in 1873
ESTABLISHED A 7-YEAR TERM
OF OFFICE FOR ALL FUTURE
PRESIDENTS OF HIS COUNTRY
*WHEN HE REFUSED TO ACCEPT
A 10-YEAR TERM*

EVERY SUBMARINE
BUILT BY PIONEER
AMERICAN INVENTOR SIMON LAKE
*WAS EQUIPPED WITH WHEELS
-SO IT COULD RIDE ALONG
THE BOTTOM OF THE SEA*

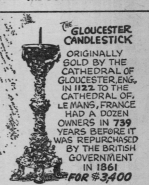

THE
**GLOUCESTER
CANDLESTICK**
ORIGINALLY
SOLD BY THE
CATHEDRAL OF
GLOUCESTER, ENG.,
IN 1122 TO THE
CATHEDRAL OF
LE MANS, FRANCE
HAD A DOZEN
OWNERS IN **739**
YEARS BEFORE IT
WAS REPURCHASED
BY THE BRITISH
GOVERNMENT
IN 1861
FOR $3,400

THE **MOST DIFFICULT JIGSAW PUZZLE IN ALL HISTORY**
THE BRITISH NAVY
TO LEARN WHY THE BRITISH BOMBER, VICTOR II, CRASHED INTO THE
SEA IN 1959 *DREDGED UP 500,000 TINY FRAGMENTS OFF WALES AND
ASSEMBLED THEM TO RECREATE 70% OF THE ORIGINAL PLANE*

THE STRUCTURE THAT DOES ITS OWN HOUSEKEEPING
— THE OAK BEAMS SUPPORTING THE BELL CAGE OF CURFEW TOWER, in the Palace of Windsor, England, *MYSTERIOUSLY REPEL EVERY TYPE OF INSECT AND NEVER GATHER DUST!*

JEAN-BAPTISTE GRESSET
(1709-1777) of Paris, France, SCORED SO WELL IN HIS ENTRANCE EXAMINATION AT THE COLLEGE OF LOUIS LE GRAND THAT INSTEAD OF BEING ACCEPTED AS A STUDENT *HE WAS INSTALLED AS A PROFESSOR-AT THE AGE OF 17*

THE **CHURCH BELL** of Lyons-la-Foret, France, RINGING THE ANGELUS IN 1573, SAVED THE LIVES OF 3 SOLDIERS LOST IN THE FOREST BY GUIDING THEM TO SAFETY *IN GRATITUDE THEY DONATED A SUM LARGE ENOUGH TO MAKE SURE THAT THE BELL WOULD RING 33 TIMES EACH NIGHT- TO COMMEMORATE CHRIST'S 33 YEARS ON EARTH - FOR THE NEXT 328 YEARS*

Paulus HERSTORFER

ACCORDING TO THE OFFICIAL
STATISTICS OF THE PARISH
OF ESTERNBERG, AUSTRIA,
DIED ON OCT. 2, 1690 AT
THE AGE OF 189

THE **TALLEST PAGODA** in Nepal
DIDN'T COST A CENT

KING BHUPATINDRA
PERSONALLY HAULED THE
FIRST 3 STONES INTO
PLACE IN 1705 AND HIS
PEOPLE COMPLETED IT IN THE
BELIEF THAT IF IT WAS SO
IMPORTANT A PROJECT
*EVERYONE SHOULD LABOR
WITHOUT PAY*

from an
old print

THE **FIRST BULLFIGHTERS** WERE NO FIGHTERS

BULLFIGHTERS IN SPAIN
until the 13th century
ALWAYS HURLED DARTS AND
ARROWS AT THE ANIMALS
*FROM THE SAFETY
OF THE TOWN WALL*

LEAVES OF THE
MOONWORT FERN
ARE ALWAYS TILTED
*TO LESSEN THEIR
EXPOSURE TO THE
BURNING RAYS
OF THE SUN*

THE **PACIFIC GODWITS** SPEND EACH SUMMER IN SIBERIA AND EVERY WINTER IN NEW ZEALAND —FLYING 6,000 MILES ON EACH MIGRATION **2,000 MILES OVER OPEN OCEAN**

LITTLE LATTICEWORK FENCES ARE ERECTED AT INTERVALS BY SHAN TRIBESMEN of Burma *IN THE BELIEF THEY WILL TRIP UP EVIL SPIRITS*

KING GEORGE IV of England WAS CRITICIZED AS A SPENDTHRIFT *BECAUSE HE WAS THE FIRST MAN TO ORDER RIDING BOOTS SHAPED FOR EACH FOOT*— BEFORE THAT THE SAME BOOT WAS WORN ON EITHER FOOT

THE **MOURNING MINARET** Agra, India IT WAS ERECTED AT AN ANGLE SO THAT IT WOULD APPEAR TO BE *BOWING TOWARD THE TOMB OF EMPEROR AKBAR*

MANNING HALL
ON THE CAMPUS OF BROWN UNIVERSITY, IN PROVIDENCE, R.I., WAS BUILT IN 1834 AS AN EXACT, THOUGH LARGER, *REPLICA OF THE ANCIENT GREEK TEMPLE OF ARTEMIS PROPYLAEA*

HENRIK ROX (1621-1682) RENOWNED DUTCH PAINTER-AT THE HEIGHT OF HIS FAME GAVE UP ART TO SUCCEED HIS FATHER AS A FERRY-BOATMAN

GILBERT ROMME French Revolutionary leader
WHEN HE WAS SENTENCED TO THE GUILLOTINE IN 1794, PLUNGED A DAGGER INTO HIS FACE, NECK AND HEART
HIS BODY WAS TURNED OVER TO FRIENDS FOR BURIAL—BUT HE RECOVERED AND LIVED ANOTHER 35 YEARS

THE IRON GRILL
WHICH UNTIL 1860 COVERED THE DOORS OF THE CATHEDRAL OF NOTRE DAME, in Paris, France,
AND WHICH MEASURED 23 FEET IN HEIGHT AND 13 FEET IN WIDTH *WAS CREATED FROM A SINGLE BLOCK OF IRON*
EXPERTS, NOTING THAT THE GRILLWORK HAD NO SEAMS, NO APPARENT BEGINNING AND NO END, STUDIED IT IN VAIN FOR A CLUE TO HOW IT WAS MADE